THE ENNEAGRAM GUIDE TO SELF-DISCOVERY, RELATIONSHIP FULFILMENT & AWAKENING:

USING THE ENNEAGRAM FOR FINDING YOUR TRUE SELF, DEEPENING YOUR RELATIONSHIPS & PSYCHOLOGICAL GROWTH

ENNEAGRAM UNWRAPPED

BOOK TWO

PERSONALITY HUB

CONTENTS

PART TWO
YOU AND THE ENNEAGRAM

PART THREE
DEEPENING RELATIONSHIPS

PART FOUR
USING THE ENNEAGRAM FOR GROWTH IN ALL AREAS

INTRODUCTION

It just feels to me like my life has been spiraling out of control ever since my dad died, and I've fallen into this rabbit hole of despair. Nothing I try works, and at first, I thought I could just fake it until things got better, but now it's starting to affect my marriage. These were the words of my client, Sally, who had just begun our coaching program, hoping that it would save her relationships.

The words she spoke echoed loudly in my mind as I recalled a distant past where I, too, faced similar frustration over my life. Despite my knowledge and training in human behavior and personal development, the experience of loss had thrown me off my game, and I didn't know how to get myself back on track. Do you know what that's like?

I don't know you or what made you pick up this book, but I do know this. We all want to feel more in control of our emotions, future, and lives.

Happiness, health, loving relationships, a fulfilling career are things we all care about, and we seek out solutions that will enable us to achieve these things in different ways. Most people look for external solutions, but you're not like most people, are you? That's why this book has piqued your interest.

How often do you find yourself thinking, "why did I do that?" or "what would cause that person to behave in such a way?" Social conditioning has led us to believe that we are stuck in a box, and there's nothing we can do to change things, but what if I told you there was a way for you to become wholly aware of this so-called "box" and not only that - to give you techniques that can enable you to perceive above and beyond it? Would that be of interest to you?

THE KEY YOU'VE BEEN SEARCHING FOR - A SECRET THAT IS FOUND

Our society encourages us to find answers to the important questions that ring in the back of our minds (e.g., how can I feel fulfilled, happy, and at peace with myself and others? How do I feel loved, and where can I find true love? Who am I really?) in the acquisition of material possessions. Sometimes it's implied that we can find it in another or by being with another human being, so we go out and look for that other who will complete us. Soon enough, we realize that no amount of material possessions and no other human being will satisfy us. If we want to feel whole and experience real happiness, we need to look for answers elsewhere. Don't get me wrong, having your material desires manifest is fantastic and a necessary part of enjoying life. Being with someone who brings you great joy and makes you feel loved is also critical to enjoying the whole human experience. But these aren't the foundation of a fulfilled life; they add to it. The foundation of a full, healthy, happy, satisfying life begins with a clear, deep understanding of yourself.

INTRODUCTION

So how much of yourself do you really understand?

Do you know the proper diet, lifestyle, career, romantic partnership, and friendships for you? How aligned do you feel with your purpose?

Let me share why this is important. Think about the most basic and trendy topic in the marketplace today, weight loss. It's a trillion-dollar industry with new fads and diets coming out every day. Many people want to lose weight so let's assume for argument's sake that you'd like to drop a few pounds before next summer. Which diet or workout program do you go for? A quick search online, and you'll realize the options are overwhelming. Each one claims that it will give you that magic solution to finally get you that six-pack you've always secretly desired. Regardless of which product you pick, there's likely a ton of testimonials from happy customers who successfully shed their belly fat in record time. That doesn't guarantee that you'd get the same results. As a matter of fact, you might purchase a particular product with high hopes only to end up feeling frustrated and disappointed by the lack of results at the end of the thirty days. You might have liked the guru that convinced you to buy the product in the first place, and he sure looked ripped and healthy, but if by the end you don't look anything like him, does that make the man a scammer?

Most people would argue yes. But this is where I want to share the first nugget of wisdom that one can only learn through this Enneagram quest.

Weight loss, like everything else, is dependent on far more than a particular diet or workout routine. Unless and until the root issues resulting in the weight gain are addressed, you will find no lasting solution. It really doesn't matter how much effort one puts in or how great the program is. When gurus offer prescriptions and solutions for personal development, health, or business success, the advice is often predicated on practices that have worked well for those individuals. And that same advice will likely work just as well for someone with similar psychological makeup. In other words, there has to be a "match" of some sort. To better understand what makes a good match, we need to dive into the topic of personality. We are all unique as human beings with varying personalities. Recent reports in infant development and brain research have suggested that fundamental variations in temperament among various types of people possess a biological basis. As such, sound advice for one person may prove disastrous for another. Now, I know that it might seem like understanding other people is impossible, but this is where things get interesting. If we only make assumptions of others based on their surface-level personality traits, it would be hard to understand or even get along with those who aren't like you, and trust me when I say this; no one is exactly like you. But if we could focus on the layers beneath the surface, we can find a lot more substance that connects and groups us in ways that foster more harmonious interactions. So, in other words, instead of looking for any weight loss solution or picking one because the guru is famous, you'd look for a solution that aligns with your psychological makeup.

The filter through which we experience life

The primary filter we use to discover ourselves and the world around us—the thing that dictates how we show up, react, and even love—is our psychology. Our desires and yearnings might sound similar, e.g., freedom, health, happiness, and love but the way they are conveyed and expressed will be diverse and far more specific depending on the filter through which we look at all of life. Modern experts prefer to use the term personality type, and so it is this filter that we are most concerned about in this book. Because after a lot of digging, I've learned that an essential factor for great relationships and understanding oneself and others is this one thing - which type are you? It's not about race, religion, sexual orientation, or cultural traditions. All these are just add-ons that magnify that underlying psychological type. When I understand your filter, we have a much better chance of getting along regardless of external differences. That's what the Ennea-gram was designed to do. It's a tool that helps us spot out filters more clearly. We learn about our core internal issues and our interpersonal strengths and deficiencies. The Enneagram is not focused on your date of birth or any external attributes but rather on your psychological makeup and behavior. It won't just point out your personality type but also the core of who you are and who you can become.

If you've been looking for a way to uncover, discover and tap into your fullest potential so you can unlock the greatness you can feel lies within you, then you've landed on the right material. And if you're here simply because, just like my client, something feels off, and you want to tack an action step that could get you back on track, then this is also the right place to be. In your hands, you now hold the only book you'll ever need to learn about and under-stand the Enneagram and how you can use this tool to transform every area of your life. That's what it did for me, that's what it's done for countless others, and if you let it, you'll reap the same benefits. Buckle up because this is going to be a fantastic ride!

PART ONE
THE ENNEAGRAM TOOL

CHAPTER I

INTRODUCING THE ENNEAGRAM TOOL

A s far back as the 4th century, we find ideas relating to the Enneagram tool, although some might argue against this. Perhaps it wasn't referred to by the same term, and it definitely didn't resemble the device we know and use today, but it's safe to assume the Enneagram model has been around for a long time. And that's one of the reasons it's a trusted model. Being both an old and modern tool, the wisdom and holistic approach involved in this self-exploration make it possible for you to finally learn the right way to observe and let go of worrisome practices and reactions. It gives you a spiritual wake-up call if you're ready to dive deeper into that exploration, but even if you're not, you still get as much as you need to continue improving yourself as a whole being.

WHAT EXACTLY IS THE ENNEAGRAM TOOL?

According to Wikipedia, Enneagram (pronounced Any-a-gram) is a model of the human psyche, principally understood and taught as a typology of nine interconnected personality types. The

Enneagram is represented in the form of a geometric model symbolizing a map, which makes sense when one learns that in the Greek language, ennéa means nine and grámma means something written or drawn.

The enneagram figure is typically composed of three parts, as you shall see in chapter three, where we'll dive into the details of this ennea diagram.

To fully grasp the power of the Enneagram, you'll need to open your mind to new ideas and suspend all unbelief and limited thoughts regarding life and who you really are. You will also need to turn up the volume of curiosity so you can start asking questions like, what is my personality? Is there more to me than just my personality? How do I figure out what my real nature is, and how do I improve the areas of my character that I don't enjoy?

If you've already been asking these questions, that's excellent because the Enneagram is a perfect personality typing and personal development tool to help answer these questions and so much more.

How many other models are there?

If you're not aware, the Enneagram model isn't the only one in the market. Other personality typing models like the Myers-Briggs Type Indicator (MBTI), DISC, and Social Styles are also used. Similar to how MBTI, DISC, and Social Styles describe typical behavior meaning, the Enneagram teaches how different personality types behave and how to recognize these behaviors in ourselves and others. But here's where the Enneagram differs, in my opinion. It doesn't just leave things at that psychological surface level and instead integrates the spiritual aspect of our nature as well. By the very basis that it's derived from ancient teaching that views development as progressive integration and upward movement within one's type, it does far more than just talking about the inductive clusters of characteristics that we would find in the results of a research investigation. In other words, the Enneagram identifies why we do what we do, i.e., the motivation for our behavior. It looks at basic fears and desires as key drivers for behavior. Since these fears and desires are often subconscious or even unconscious, this process of discovering your true self using the Enneagram tool becomes more of a quest instead of a standardized report. And when we bond to the Enneagram, we get a simple idea planted inside that we are far more than just personality types. We are, in fact, spiritual beings incarnated through the material world.

Is it religious?

Absolutely not. This isn't about religion because the Enneagram sets itself apart from all doctrinal differences. People from every religion, creed, and walk of life have benefited from using this tool. It doesn't matter whether you identify as a devout catholic, Christian, Muslim, atheist, Mormon, Jew, man, woman, LGBTQ, rich, poor, black, white, or brown this tool can work for you. As you dive into the structure and workings of this tool, you'll realize that all Enneagram type Sixes are pretty much the same every-where in the world. So, a devout Catholic who is a type Six is a great deal more like the Sixes who are Muslim than they could imagine. And that goes for every other type. In the end, it changes our perspective, and we realize how similar we are all at that deeper, more human level, creating a lot more compassion and empathy across the world. Just imagine how different our world could be and how many misunderstandings, wrongdoings, and pain we could obliterate if more of us realized just how similar we are from those we tend to discriminate against.

CHAPTER 2

THE ORIGINS

T he mystery surrounding the Enneagram and its origins continue to gather much speculation and dispute for practitioners. While it is good to question the authenticity of this tool, and I'll do my best to offer some insights, don't allow that curiosity to turn into doubt. History around the Enneagram is clouded somewhat (like many ancient tools), but the model's effectiveness as a framework and a map for self-discovery stands solid.

So what's the actual origin of the Enneagram, and can we say with absolute certainty where it came from?

Well, here's what we do know. It is connected to different spiritual and oral traditions and certain philosophical and mathematical traditions. Some others believe that variations of the Enneagram symbol can be traced to the sacred geometry of Pythagorean mathematicians and mystical mathematics. Plotinus, in the Enneads, speaks of the nine divine qualities that manifest in human nature. We also see variations of the Enneagram symbol appear in the Sufi tradition, with specific reference to the

Naqshbandi Order. It may have also entered into esoteric Judaism through the philosopher Philo, later becoming embedded into the branches of the Tree of Life in the Kabbalah. There's a possible relationship with Christianity through medieval references to Evagrius' catalog of various forms of temptation (Logismoi), which much later, in medieval times, was translated into the seven deadly sins. The Franciscan mystic Ramon Llull taught philosophy and theology of nine principles in an attempt to integrate different faith traditions, and in a 17th-century text, we find an Enneagram-like drawing made by Jesuit mathematician Athanasius Kircher (Adopted from Wagner, 2010).

THE MODERN INTEGRATIVE VERSION OF THE ENNEAGRAM

The evolution of the Enneagram as we know it today took place recently in the 21st century. A Russian mystic and teacher named George Gurdjieff reintroduced this antiquated symbol in form and shape that we identify as the Enneagram diagram (to be discussed in detail in chapter 3). Only Gurdjieff did not draw it out but instead taught it primarily through a series of sacred dances or movements. He believed it was better when people directly sensed the meaning of the symbol and the processes it represents. Although Gurdjieff's teaching did not include a system of personality types associated with the symbol (that came later through another contributor, as you'll see shortly), he did reveal to advanced students that we all have what he termed "chief feature." This chief feature is the lynchpin of a person's ego structure and is the fundamental characteristic that defines that individual. When asked where he learned about the Enneagram, he said he was introduced to it during a visit to a monastery in Afghanistan in the 1920s, but nothing more is disclosed regarding the origin of this symbol. What we do know is that since then,

Oscar Ichazo took the helm of the Enneagram studies and coined the term "Enneagram of Personality." Ichazo is credited as the person who originally put the system together in the way we use it today. This Bolivian-born teacher and healer, who also spent a significant portion of his early years in Peru, first moved to Buenos Aires in Argentina to learn from a school of inner work. Thereafter he journeyed to Asia to gather more knowledge before returning to South America, where he began putting together a systematic approach to all he'd learned. After many years of study, research, and practice, Ichazo created the Arica School (founded in 1968) as a means of sharing the knowledge he'd received over the years. In the 1970s, while living in Chile, Ichazo received a group of noted psychologists and writers from America who wanted to study and experience first hand the methods of attaining self-realization at Arica. Among these individuals were Claudio Naranjo and John Lilly (The Enneagram Institute).

The end result of weeks spent at the Arica School studying with Ichazo was the introduction of this tool into America and the rest of the world where modern psychology was in practice. Individuals such as Ochs, Almaas, and Maitri studied with Claudio Naranjo. Ochs introduced the Enneagram to the Christian communities in the United States, which got authors like Jerry Wagner, Don Riso, and Russ Hudson excited to further spread the teachings of the Enneagram (Integrative9 History of the Enneagram). Thanks to these contemporary theorists, our knowledge and development of the Enneagram tools continue to grow far beyond what anyone, including Ichazo (who passed away in 2020), could have foreseen.

IS IT SCIENTIFIC OR MYSTICAL?

There's no binary answer to this question. Given how popular and highly recommended this tool has become in personal development and professional settings, we cannot label it purely scientific or mystical. I like to think it's a little bit of both. While the Enneagram system as we know it dates back to the '60s when Ichazo started teaching it, the philosophy behind this tool contains components from all traditions that stretch back thousands of years. That's why we can confidently employ it to help us unlock our hidden potential, uncover our blind spots and enable us to grow in every area of life. Use the following chapters as clues that allow you to discover who you really are so you can feel more in charge of your destiny and your life story. The best part is that the more you know yourself, the easier it becomes to understand and predict other people's behavior.

The American Version of the Enneagram versus the original system taught by Ichazo:

Ichazo taught a system of 108 Enneagrams, but the American movement spearheaded by Claudio Naranjo, who still teaches the Enneagram to date, was based on the first four of the Enneagrams. These are called the Enneagrams of the Passions, the Enneagrams of the Virtues, the Enneagram of the Fixations, and the Enneagram of the Holy Ideas. Why were they categorized like this? In an interview with Ichazo, he said, "We have to distinguish between a man as he is in essence and as he is in ego or personality. In essence, every person is perfect, fearless, and in loving unity with the entire cosmos; there is no conflict within the person between head, heart, and stomach or between the person and others. Then something happens; the ego begins to develop, karma accumulates, there is a transition from objectivity to subjectivity; man falls from essence to personality." (Interviews with Ichazo, page 9)

WHAT ARE VIRTUES, PASSIONS, HOLY IDEAS, AND FIXATIONS ABOUT?

Later in the book, we'll name the virtues for each Enneagram type so you can see what your higher self is calling you toward in this lifetime.

According to Ichazo's theory, holy ideas and virtues are our higher spiritual qualities, and when these become distorted by the ego, they become fixations (head)and passions (heart), respectively. This relationship between the higher self and the ego is the real work we must undertake. That's what our self-discovery quest is all about.

Approaching this book and the Enneagram with the desire to label yourself a particular personality just because it feels good is wasted effort and a missed understanding of what this tool was intended for. Your purpose in self-discovery should be to bring about that balance between your ego and higher self that's been missing. The more you feel like you've lost your center and become distorted in your thinking, feeling, and behavior, the more you need to work on that relationship with self. Use your increasing self-awareness to recognize the patterns of distortion obscuring your connection and creating disharmony in your life. Get to know your type so you can direct your inner work and facil-itate the transformation that's waiting to happen within you.

If you realize that your virtues are off, don't force yourself to become a virtuous person. It doesn't work like that. To become virtuous, we need to relax, reconnect with our higher self and become more awake so we can see through the fears and desires of our ego. Only then will virtuous qualities naturally manifest. And when it comes to reconciling our thoughts about passion, realize that having desires isn't bad. Passions merely point us to an underlying reality that something is missing; we've lost something, and we need to get it back. The thing we need to work on getting back in order to heal, make whole, and satiate that passion isn't what we usually chase after. Our ego might distort our thinking and cause us to work ourselves to death, sacrificing everything in our path just to become powerful, successful, or to be loved by another, thinking that will make us complete. Yet, once we're there, the emptiness still exits. This is one of the cornerstones Ichazo wanted his students to grasp. The misguided coping strategies that our ego uses under the disguise of passion are but a distortion of inherent essential virtue. What we're in search of is restoring contact with our Essential nature and our true identity as Spirit.

The other big idea here is that an individual's ego fixation is rooted in losing one's holy idea. We lose the ability to recognize the unity of being. We become stuck in duality and segregation, and our mind is constantly storming. Similar to what we've learned about virtue and passions when we become disconnected from our higher self, that sense of freedom that we innately know we should have turned into an ego-fixation.

However, all of these can be restored as we use the Enneagram knowledge to work on ourselves. How deep you want to go in this journey is up to you, but I can assure you, the deeper you go, the richer, more fulfilling, and enjoyable this human experience will become.

CHAPTER 3
THE ENNEAGRAM DIAGRAM

To use the Enneagram tool effectively, one must learn to read it accurately. This chapter will give you an overview of all the nine Enneagram Types, offer a visual illustration of the Enneagram diagram and its parts, and then teach you how to read the diagram. Only then will you be ready to dive into the details of each Enneagram type.

There are nine personality types that are placed around the Enneagram diagram, namely, The Reformer, The Helper, The Achiever, The Individualist, The Investigator, The Loyalist, The Enthusiast, The Challenger, and The Peacemaker.

Each of the enneatypes represents an archetype and worldview that the particular type identifies with. It's their home base and the framework through which they think, feel, act and relate to their environment, other people, and themselves. But this is far more than just personality profiling. In fact, if you only use the Enneagram to spot personalities, you might be disappointed when you discover that different enneatypes may display similar behavior. That's because the Enneagram model works under the premise that behavior alone isn't enough to tell you who a person really is. As a matter of fact, it teaches that outward behavior can be deceiving when trying to figure out people or even the effectiveness of this tool for self-discovery. You should therefore identify yourself and others by exploring motivation. Become more curious about "why" you or another chooses to act in a certain way. That's the real value of using this model and the best way to discover why we do what we do in life.

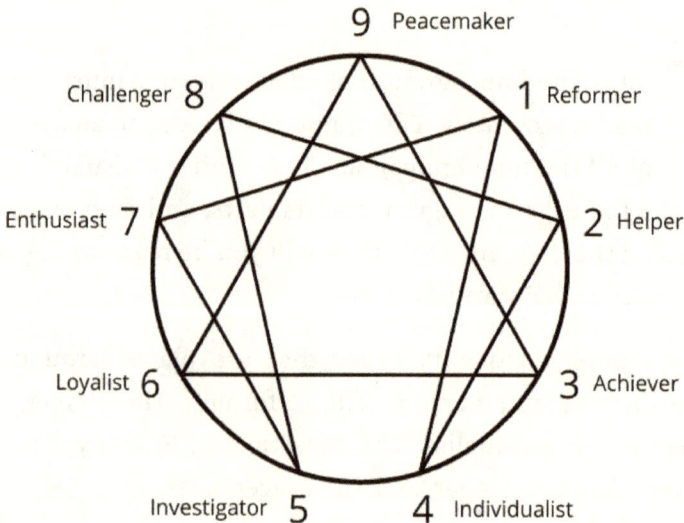

9 Peacemaker

Challenger 8   1 Reformer

Enthusiast 7   2 Helper

Loyalist 6   3 Achiever

Investigator 5   4 Individualist

CHAPTER 4

UNDERSTANDING THE ENNEAGRAM SYMBOL

The modern-day Enneagram symbol is drawn as a geometrical shape with nine points. There's an outer circle on which the nine points that represent the nine personality types are numbered clockwise. The Enneagram uses a horizontal system to designate a number to each type, so no one number is better than another.

Inside the circle, there's a triangle between points 9, 3, and 6 and an irregular hexagon that connects all other points. If you're wondering what the circle represents, teachers of the Enneagram have said it represents the wholeness and unity of human life, i.e., the essence of life. The inner shapes represent the divisions, yet even with that, we can still see points of connections. This is important to remember as you go through your self-discovery. While you might be different from all the other types, you are still connected and form part of the whole.

9

8   1

7   2

6   3

5   4

You'll find what we call wings on either side of each point (per-sonality). Enneagram teachings tell us that wings represent related personality styles that lie dormant within us. We can choose to transition into a quality or mute a character trait that belongs to either of the wings our type is connected to and, in so doing, develop new facets of ourselves. For example, an Ennea-gram type One has the Nine and Two wing on either side. Type One can pull qualities from either the Enneagram Nine (The Peacemaker) or the Enneagram Two (The Giver). We'll be identi-fying each Enneagram type's wing in an upcoming chapter as well as how they may impact a person's behavior and personality.

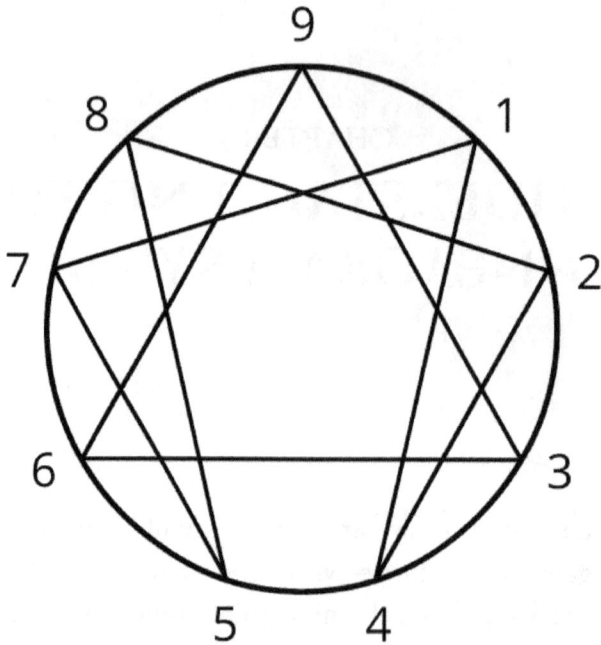

HOW THE MODERN ENNEAGRAM WORKS

If you're a beginner on this journey of self-discovery, you'll find this section of the book especially helpful because it breaks down the fundamentals you need to focus on to get the most out of the Enneagram tool. Although the Enneagram can be quite complex, this is what you need to know at the beginning of your studies. Further knowledge and understanding will unravel as you get deeper into your quest and through the daily use of this tool.

The first thing you need to learn is your basic personality type. Each of us will identify strongly with one of the nine Enneagram personality types, depending on the motives and fears that drive us. One's primary type is influenced by biological and environmental factors, including but not limited to the family dynamic, parental relationships, childhood trauma, and any other significant occurrences during those formative years.

You'll likely find that you naturally relate more to one type than any other. The consensus is that people do not change from one Enneagram personality type to another. Instead, they resonate with different traits depending on their overall level of development and psychological and spiritual health.

The second thing you need to learn about is your wings. You'll see there are two wings associated with your personality type, as well as different levels of development for your specific type. You'll also get guidance on the directions your type can take, which could either lead to integration and growth or disintegration and stress.

The other super important thing you need to learn about are the three Centers of intelligence and the three instincts that drive all types. Becoming aware of the key motivations and fears that mainly guide your actions and decisions will give you increased self-awareness and the chance to make shifts in your personality.

Only then can you correctly type yourself and others. Remember, you must refrain from making assumptions about yourself and others purely through behavior and enneatype. Go deeper and uncover the instincts and levels of development first before determining which type you or anyone else is. Before we dive into each personality type, let's look a little more closely at the three centers and instincts.

THE CENTERS OF INTELLIGENCE

The Enneagram model is a 3 X 3 arrangement of nine personality types in the three Centers (Enneagram Institute). These centers are broken down into intellect, instinct, and intuition. This triad is based on how we habitually process and respond to each other and life in general. Let's get into a little scientific talk before you label the notion too *woo woo* for you. Neurobiologists have discovered that the human body has three "centers" where many nerve cells bundle together to serve the nervous system and pass information more efficiently. These centers are found in the head, chest, and gut or lower abdomen. Enneagram teachers worked with these three centers long before scientists formally proved them, and they termed them "centers of intelligence." In the context of the Enneagram, this triad enables us to understand the basic emotions that motivate various Enneatypes, all grouped within that 3X3 model.

Some teachers prefer to label them the thinking center (head), instinctive center (gut), and feeling center (heart). We tend to discuss this particular triad, even though there are many more because this one's easy for beginners to grasp. Although we have all three centers of intelligence, one is usually more dominant. Knowing whether you're in the thinking, feeling, or instinctive center can help you accurately determine your personality type. That can be especially useful when you're torn between a few types.

The Enneagram personality types are divided into three groups, as shown in the diagram below. The Instinctive center has enneatypes 1,8,9; the Feeling Center has 2,3,4, and the Thinking Center has 5,6,7.

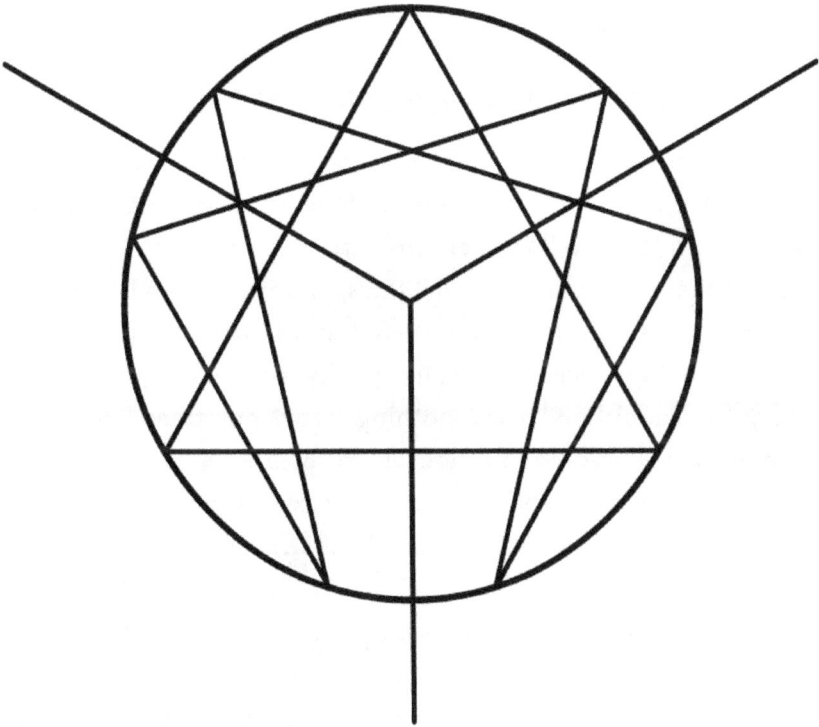

How did the original teachers of this system come up with these particular groupings? They believed that each type results from a specific relationship with a cluster of issues that characterize that center. Simply put, when you lose contact with your higher self, unconscious emotional responses arise from within, and until you can resolve these issues, these emotions become the default reaction.

So, in the Thinking Center (head), the unresolved emotion is fear. For the Feeling Center (heart), the emotion is shame, and for the Instinctive/body Center (gut), the emotion is anger or sometimes rage. That's not to say one only experiences the emotion associated with their center of intelligence because, as you know, we all feel shame, anger, and fear. Instead, the lesson here is that one of these emotions affects us most. It is a common theme that seems to follow us everywhere.

An illustration might help solidify this idea

I have a friend who grew up in the worst of conditions. Today she's a well-known Instagram influencer specializing in DIY fashion and vintage knitwear. She's been featured in magazines and speaks across the United States, motivating and inspiring young girls, especially those growing up in poor neighborhoods. Although her life seems almost like a fairytale, her early childhood and young adulthood were nothing but a nightmare. She was born into a single-parent household where there was barely enough money for food. Her uncles sexually abused her, and when her mom remarried, the new husband also abused her. She ran away by the age of sixteen, lived on the streets of California for a while before meeting someone, getting pregnant, and finding herself repeating that same cycle of abuse. It took a really long time for her to finally land a healthy, non-abusive relationship. However, through this Enneagram tool and extensive self-discovery work, she was able to start making permanent changes.

When my friend tried to identify her personality type, she was torn between three types, but after learning about the centers of intelligence and realizing that her theme was predominantly shame and that this theme has been following her like a dark shadow recreating the same nightmares she had as a child, that's when it a lightbulb went on. Things have never been the same since.

Hence when it comes to your center of intelligence, the idea is to observe your life and determine which emotional theme is most dominant and recurring. Let's explore each center with a little more detail:

The Thinking/Head Center:

The Thinking Center aligns with types 5, 6, and 7. The Enneagram numbers might seem different, and, indeed, their outer behavior and personality traits differ from one number to the next. However, these three types all share the same "thinking," in the sense that their most dominant approach to life is thinking with their head rather than listening to intuition or gut feelings. These are the people who tend to be "too much in their head" when processing information or reacting to conditions.

All type 5s, 6s, and 7s are very concerned with strategies and seek out security and safety above all else. Their biggest underlying issue and a theme that recurs throughout their human experience until resolved is fear. Although they all deal with fear and anxiety, how they deal with it is very different due to their diverse personality traits. You'll find that Fives will be anxious and apprehensive about the outside world and thus prefer to isolate themselves. The Sixes handle their anxiety by suppressing it, which manifests as internal stress, wild imagination, and a lot of pessimistic "worst-case scenario" thinking. They are the most fearful in the group and sometimes struggle to trust their own thoughts. That causes them to constantly seek external approval and validation. The Sevens deal with fear and anxiety by denial and avoidance. They already have the sense that there's too much pain, loss, deprivation, and fear within them, but they don't want to deal with it, so, instead, they do everything possible to stimulate their minds with things that excite them. This is manifested by constant busyness and physical distractions so their minds and bodies won't deal with the inner restlessness and fear they're suppressing.

The Feeling/Heart Center:

The Feeling Center aligns with Enneagram types 2, 3, and 4. As mentioned before, the thing that connects these seemingly different types is a layer deeper than personality traits or outer behavior. Instead, it's the fact that they process life predominantly through emotions. If you've been around someone who likes to say, "It just doesn't feel right to me, so I can't do," or, "I didn't hire her because something about her didn't feel right," then you've interacted with a heart-centered individual. Maybe you're that person, in which case you'll finally understand why a particular emotion lingers no matter what you do. Enneagram type Twos, Threes, and Fours are mainly concerned with how others perceive them, and they really love getting attention. The underlying issue that has to be resolved is a feeling of shame.

How does each type handle its recurring issue?

Twos tend to focus on doing things that appear to make them feel better, but that really just mask or mute out their inner shame. They want to convince themselves that they are good, loving people by focusing on positive feelings for others while repressing their unwanted feelings. In relationships, this creates a very fragile connection; as long as the Two gets positive emotional responses from the other person, they will feel wanted and somehow manage to tame that feeling of shame, but it is very conditional.

Threes are more resistant to their inner feeling of shame, and they try to deny this emotion as much as possible. In this group, Threes are the most out of touch with their feelings of shame and inadequacy. They use coping mechanisms and find objective ways to stave off their shame. Fours are more introspective. They are aware of their dark side, so they try to control it by burying it as deep as they can and turning their focus to how unique and special they are. As a general rule of thumb, you'll find Fours to be highly creative, and they use this ability to deal with shameful feelings. Unfortunately, they are also the most likely to succumb to feelings of inadequacy and take drastic measures to escape that unwanted reality.

THE INSTINCTIVE/BODY/GUT CENTER:

The gut center aligns with types 8, 9, and 1. These Enneagram types couldn't be more different in personality, but one thing they have in common is they really do listen to their gut instinct. That's how they make decisions, process information, and deal with difficulties in life. Eight's Nines and Ones are very concerned with justice, they love having autonomy, and one of the main underlying issues which can sometimes be hard to spot is anger. When you hear someone say, "I only use my gut to make any decision in life," you can be sure that person falls into this triad. And even if their logic or thinking tells them something different, they'll still go with what the gut tells them to do.

How do these different personality types deal with their unresolved anger?

Well, the Eights seem to be the easiest ones to spot because they don't hide their anger. They'd love to control it, and in fact, some do a pretty good job, but with a type Eight, you'll outwardly see displays of anger quite regularly. They tend to be quite "temperamental" or hot-tempered. Nines are in denial over their anger issues, so they try to suppress it because they don't want to come across as temperamental and upset anyone. In their desire to be good, they'd rather avoid owning that they have this negative emotion. Among the three types, Nines are the most out of touch with their anger and often feel threatened by it. Ones are pretty intriguing because they care so much about achieving perfection (and, of course, view anger as imperfection) and control that they cope by doing their best to repress this emotion.

In section II of this book, you'll discover some suggestions for resolving whatever dominant emotion you might be noticing in your life.

THE WINGS AND LEVELS OF DEVELOPMENT

As you start learning the various classifications, you'll notice there are certain qualities not on your dominant type that you resonate with. The wings are the two adjacent types located next to your primary personality type. The wings typically complement and support or at times contradict your basic type, giving you that overall personality that you identify with. You can think of this as the "second side" of your personality, and it also influences who you are. That's why it's good to know your wings and how they impact your behavior and life experience. How many wings can one have? Some schools of thought claim one, and others claim we have two wings.

Given that there are two adjacent types for each number, I reckon two wings make sense. However, one wing might

24

resonate stronger when you assess the qualities, and that's okay. Experts on the matter say most people have a dominant wing, causing the other to be less visible. You'll get to see the different wings and what they represent for each type when we break down the types and subtypes over the following three chapters.

One last thing we need to mention here is the levels of development. A continuum of behaviors, motivations, and attitudes exists within each personality type that all come together to express a complete personality. A type Nine can be at different levels of development at various stages of their life. The same is true for all the other types. What's even more intriguing is that you and your friend could both identify as the same type but realize you're at differing levels of development. In 1977, Don Riso originally discovered and worked out all the traits that comprise each type, and further developed them, in collaboration with Hudson, in the 1990s. They are the only Enneagram teachers to include this critical factor in their treatment of the Enneagram (Enneagram Institute).

The levels are divided into healthy, average, and unhealthy traits. Think of this as a skeletal structure that enables you to dive deeper into any particular type to understand where they are in their journey and how far they need to go to unlock their highest potential. Each level helps us understand how any particular type is aligned with Presence, so the more aligned a person is, the better they will function and the higher they will be in their development. You may assume that the healthy levels of development indicate that the individual has achieved spiritual liberation and is no longer bound by the ego. Therefore, the lowest and unhealthiest level indicates that a person has lost their contact and connection to their higher self and feels the most constricted, bound vigorously by the ego. Such a person would be caught up in the fixations of their particular type and ruled by their basic fears and desires.

As you get to know your type, pay close attention to the level of development you most identify with. Be candid with yourself. Only then can you recognize the inner work that needs to take place.

CHAPTER 5

ENNEAGRAM PERSONALITY TYPING SYSTEM PART 1

TYPE 1: THE PERFECTIONIST OR THE REFORMER

Overview of type One:

Type Ones are called perfectionists because they live based on an ideology of perfection, order, and constant improvement both of themselves and those around them. Ones love rules and have a powerful sense of right and wrong. They need to feel like they have everything under control at all times. They will be very professional and objective at work and pay lots of attention to details and quality standards. Different types of Ones will view the world based on their level of development, but as a general rule of thumb, while healthy Ones see an abundance of situations that aren't quite right based on their ideals, they accept things just as they are. Despite their strong sense of justice and fairness, they are serene enough to tolerate and understand diversity in humanity. Average Ones are more rigid and less accepting. They compartmentalize as a coping mechanism and might suppress emotions to follow their strict ideals. Unhealthy ones have so disconnected from their higher self that their qualities become negative. Their rigidity and inability to accept those that don't match up to their ideals creates a lot of condemnation, anger, and disdain for humanity and the world in general.

Within the Centers of Intelligence triad, type Ones fall into the "gut" center where anger is the core emotion to resolve.

A healthy type One will come across as responsible, ethical, idealistic, earnest, self-disciplined, orderly, and conscientious. These are actually pretty distinct qualities that one would easily observe in type Ones.

You'll also recognize that they typically have very high standards, which is great until it's not. When things don't go as planned or if people don't meet their high expectations, Ones can become resentful, impatient, and highly critical.

At their best, though, Ones are pretty noble and wise. Some might even say they possess the ability to be morally heroic in their attitudes and behavior.

Core Desire: Type One's desire to be good, perfect, and live with integrity.

Core Fear: Their greatest fear is to become dishonorable or corrupted by evil. They are so afraid of being flawed or "bad."

What motivates type Ones? A type One wants the world and everyone around them to be the best and do so correctly. The strong urge is to be good and honorable and to live by their ideals beyond criticism so that no one can find fault.

Wings:

Type One has the Nine-Wing, which is "The Idealist," and the Two-Wing, which is "The Advocate."

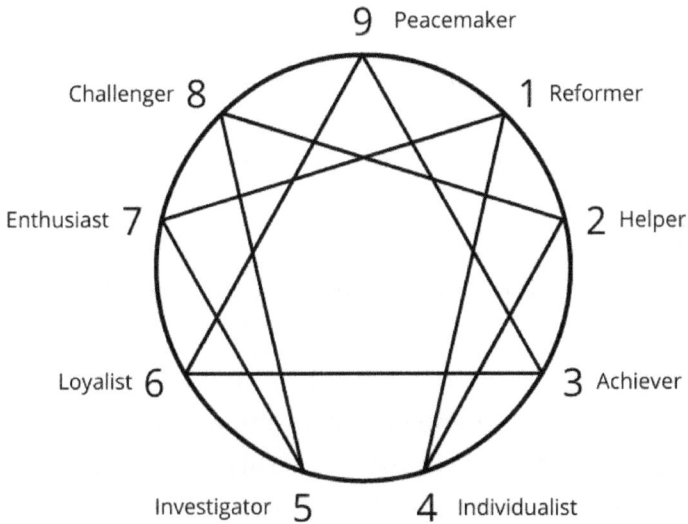

The type has two arrows, namely 4 and 7. When moving in the direction of disintegration and stress (four), Ones become moody, irrational, and too judgemental. However, the arrow pointing to growth and integration (seven) shows an angry, critical One transforming into a more spontaneous and joyful individual like a healthy Seven.

Examples of famous people:

Some well-known people sharing the Enneagram type One include Kate Middleton, Michelle Obama, Hillary Clinton, Nelson Mandela, Prince Charles, Martha Stewart, Osama bin Laden, Celine Dion, Jerry Seinfeld, Jane Fonda, Meryl Steep, and George Harrison.

Type one levels of development:

There are different expressions of type Ones that you'll need to learn. At various stages of development, a type One will exhibit certain behavior and attitudes depending on how disconnected they are from their higher Self. Let's look at each level.

Healthy levels

Level 1 is when the type One is at their best. At this point, the individual is extraordinarily wise and discerning, self-accepting, and serene. They are realistic, mission-driven, and they know the best action to take in each moment. Their interaction with others is inspiring, humane, and empathetic. This type One is highly hopeful and believes the truth always wins.

Level 2 is where type One is conscientious with strong personal convictions. The sense of right and wrong is extremely high, and this individual likes to work in a structured and systematic way adhering to all personal religious and moral values. A type One this stage of development is rational, reasonable, self-disciplined, mature, and moderate in all things.

Level 3 is still healthy, and a type One at this stage will be principles in their actions, objective, ethical and fair in all they do. This individual is very concerned with truth and justice. They have a strong sense of responsibility, personal integrity, often reaching for ways to express and share with others a higher sense of purpose, e.g., by teaching or leading a movement.

Average levels

Level 4 is the phase a type One becomes a high-minded idealist. They've become dissatisfied with reality, and they feel it's up to them to improve everything. You'll find most critics, advocates, and crusaders or Ones that are into "causes" fall under this level of development.

Level 5 is where type One becomes super rigid. Everything has to be "perfect," and they can't afford to make any mistakes. This individual is very organized and attentive but also puritanical and emotionally constricted. You'll hear words like "anal-compulsive" associated with such a person.

Level 6 type One is highly critical, judgemental, and suffers from perfectionism. Based on their perspective, they are highly opinionated about everything and the kind that will badger, interrupt and correct you in the middle of a sentence or an action just because they want you to "do the right thing." Impatience is more pronounced at this level, and you might even get a scolding look or an abrasive talk when you don't do things exactly as they desire.

Unhealthy levels

Level 7 type One is extremely self-righteous and dogmatic. They are intolerant of others and think everyone who doesn't think and act like them is wrong. At this level, the individual deals in absolutes and feel like they alone know "The Truth."

Level 8 type One is obsessed with the imperfections they see in themselves and others. The individual at this level wants everyone to fix their wrongdoings, and unfortunately, they might say one thing and do the opposite making them quite contradictory.

Level 9 is the most unhealthy and lowest level of development in type One. At this stage of development, the individual is condemnatory and cruel to themselves and others because they cannot stand the imperfections they see. The failure to live up to the ideal they deem perfect is too much to bear, and we often find such a person deeply depressed, suffering from nervous breakdowns, and even contemplating or attempting suicide.

Addictions:

To cope with and suppress some of the emotional and psychological unrest that this type faces, especially at the unhealthy levels of development, Ones may resort to Alcohol. Some, however, attempt to force their self-control by undereating, leading to bulimia or extreme diets and vitamins.

HOW TO RECOGNIZE IF YOU'RE AN ENNEAGRAM ONE

Let's look at some easy-to-spot traits for an Enneagram type One, and make sure you take note of how many you identify with. Bear in mind that some of these traits will be more pronounced in healthy Ones while others will be more present in unhealthy Ones.

- You hold yourself to extremely high standards in everything you do.
- Most people, including yourself, tend to use the term "perfectionist" or "strict" when describing you.
- You're incredibly organized, diligent, systematic, and you thrive in systems and structure.

- Rules? You love rules and believe that's the best way to get things done/
- Your communication style is direct, honest, and thoughtful.
- You like to take charge of your duties, and everyone knows you're super responsible.
- Patience isn't one of your strengths, especially when things aren't going your way.
- You work hard to control and civilize your natural impulses. Spontaneity and risk-taking sound silly and unnecessary.
- There's a super loud inner critic that you have to deal with every day, whether it's the voice of a parent or someone else, constantly criticizing you when you fail.
- Being grounded and fair is essential to you, so you do your best to detach emotions from a problem. That's especially true when the problem involves making a significant decision that impacts others.

STRUGGLES THAT TYPE ONES MIGHT HAVE

Unrealistic expectations

All Ones are driven by the need to make the world around them better and lead ethical, honest, honorable, and responsible lives. If a type One says he'll do something, then you can bet everything they will do it.

Many people respect and greatly depend on Ones because they're totally reliable, ethical, and carry themselves with great integrity. They set super high standards that only they can live up to, and it's pretty inspiring in some cases. But sometimes, these high standards can turn into a curse. The more unhealthy a type One is, the bigger this curse will be because they'll often project their own inadequacies to those around them. A type One is often their own worst critic, and even minor failures can become unbearable, causing them to take drastic measures, including self-punishment.

Taking everything too seriously

Average and unhealthy type Ones can come across as rigid, no-nonsense individuals who have little taste for fun. They just don't know how to relax and loosen up or enjoy life with a bit of spontaneity. Leisure activities seem like unnecessary and even immoral indulgences. Their self-control is somewhat forced because they don't want to deal with their emotions making it difficult for the person to express feelings naturally.

Not good enough

Average and unhealthy Ones tend to struggle with this most. They view their failures and defects as unacceptable, no matter how small. Self-judgment and criticism are high at these levels of development, causing the individual to feel defeated by life and not good enough for whatever they desire to have.

Overfilling your plate

By this, I mean taking on too much responsibility and pushing yourself to the limit. Many type Ones believe they need to carry the weight of the world on their shoulder. While that sounds really selfless, it's often not a smart idea as it creates a lot of anxiety, overwhelms, frustration, and undue stress. The need to do everything to perfection only exacerbates the matter creating feelings of guilt, especially when their high standards aren't met or if they fail at something.

GROWTH TIPS FOR ONES

#1: Give yourself permission to "play" and unlock some of your inner childhood, especially the easy-going aspects.

Allow yourself to be silly, fun, and free-spirited. Consciously choose to block out time for an activity that's fun, whether that's playing your favorite board games, dancing, painting, pottery, or simply going to the park with a friend and playing frisbee.

#2: Ask for help

It's normal for a type One to want to carry the weight of the world on their shoulder, but everyone knows we do our best work when it's a team effort. Don't burn yourself out trying to be perfect at everything. Instead, look at your current workload and the things you've been struggling with and just ask others to help. And when others come in to help, remind yourself that it's okay for them not to be perfect or do it exactly like you. They are unique and will do their best work when you give them space to do their thing.

#3: Quiet that inner critic

Your inner dialogue has to be kept in check immediately. Belittling yourself, fault finding, and dwelling too much on your weaknesses, failures, and shortcomings only destroy your self-esteem. It's time to silence that voice. It won't happen at the snap of a finger, but things will get better with practice and deliberate action to switch the conversation. Consider creating a silly avatar for that inner critic and change the tone of voice to match a cartoon character that you find hilarious. You can also practice more compassion and self-love, which we'll discuss next.

#4: Practice self-love and self-acceptance

The best way to enhance the positive qualities of your type and heal the aspects that don't serve you is to increase your self-love and acceptance. Learn to love yourself unconditionally, even the parts you don't particularly like about yourself. When that inner critic says something, respond with "thank you for bringing that to my attention. I still think I did a pretty good job."

#5: Acknowledge, embrace, process and heal your unresolved emotion

Anger doesn't serve you, so pretending it's not there only disconnects you from your higher self. Instead of repressing or suppressing anger, find healthy ways to process and heal yourself. For example, when someone hurts your feelings, don't fall into passive-aggressive behavior, let them know they've hurt you, or find another way to address it, such as writing a letter and then burning it. Or, when you feel anger brewing, find a private place where you can scream at the top of your lungs or punch your pillow until all the emotion is released.

TYPE 2: THE GIVER/HELPER

Overview of type Two:

Type Twos are called helpers because they are genuinely invested in helping others, especially at healthy levels of development. And even if they're underdeveloped, they are still highly invested in seeing themselves as helpful. Relationships matter a lot to type Twos. A sense of belonging and feeling loved is essential for a helper, which causes them to seek relationships where they can nurture, care for, and help others. They are eager to involve themselves in other people's lives and struggle with the word "No." In fact, sometimes they can agree to help someone even at their own expense because they feel the need to prove that they are dependable. Type Twos are warm, gentle, excellent team players, and radiate kindness to everyone. At work, they will be focused on building relationships, offering support, and doing their best to create a more peaceful, loving environment.

Different types of Twos will view the world based on their level of development, but as a general rule of thumb, healthy Twos are selfless and find their fulfillment through various acts of giving unconditional love. Not only do they understand the meaning of empathy, but they also embody it in their daily lives. Average Twos like to take on a martyr role in their relationships. They need constant validation and suffer significantly from people-pleasing. Unhealthy Twos are overly possessive, enjoy pity parties, and often use sympathy to get attention from people. Some become clingy and overbearing. The nurturing, generous aspect becomes poisoned and manipulative, making their intentions insincere.

Within the Centers of Intelligence triad, type Twos fall into the "heart" center where shame is the core emotion to resolve.

A healthy type Two will come across as kind, caring, compassionate, empathetic, gentle, patient, supportive, and loving. These are actually pretty distinct qualities that one would easily observe in type Twos. You might also notice they tend to be huge people-pleasers, especially at the lower levels of development.

At their best, Twos are considerate, generous, loving, and people-centered. They know their self-worth and strike a healthy balance between selfless service and tending to their own growth and needs.

Core Desire: Type Twos want to be appreciated, valued, and wanted. They have a strong need to belong and to be loved.

Core Fear: Type Twos fear rejection, losing love, or being unlovable.

What motivates type Twos? The need to belong and be desired by others. Twos want to feel needed, and they often look to others to express agreement and vindicate their claims about their goodness.

Wings:

Type Two has the One-Wing, which is "The Servant," and the Three-Wing, which is "The Host/Hostess."

Arrows and their meaning:

The type has two arrows, namely 8 and 4. When moving in the direction of disintegration and stress (eight), Twos are needy, possessive, highly aggressive, and dominating in their relationships. They have unhealthy levels of pride. However, the arrow pointing to growth and integration (four) shows us that a prideful, self-deceptive Two can transform into a more self-nurturing and emotionally aware individual like a healthy Four.

Examples of famous people:

Some well-known people sharing the Enneagram type Two include Mother Theresa, Maya Angelou, Eleanor Roosevelt, Monica Lewinsky, Luciano Pavarotti, Lionel Richie, Elizabeth Taylor, Bishop Desmond Tutu, Paula Abdul, Priscilla Presley, Dolly Parton, and Paramahansa Yogananda.

Type Two levels of development:

There are different expressions of type Twos that you'll need to learn. At various stages of development, type Two will exhibit certain behavior and attitudes depending on how disconnected they are from their higher Self. Let's look at each level.

Healthy levels

Level 1 is a type Two and their best. An individual operating at this level is altruistic, deeply unselfish, and humble. This person genuinely loves unconditionally and finds a healthy balance between loving and giving themselves to others and self-care. This type Two freely gives without expectation and feels it's a privilege to be in the lives of others and to have the power to nurture such powerful relationships. The connection with the higher self is optimum, and this type Two knows that feels that in giving to others, they are in fact giving to the whole.

Level 2 is where type Two naturally radiates empathy, thoughtfulness, forgiveness, and compassion for others. They are very concerned with the needs of others and are sincere in their attempts to care for and love others.

Level 3 is where type Two focuses more on serving others, praising, appreciating, and finding good in others. They are generous and absolutely reliable, yet they still know how to strike that balance between taking care of others and tending to their own needs.

Average levels

Level 4 is where type Two falls into the trap of people-pleasing in an attempt to be seen as helpful and reasonable. They become overly friendly, emotionally demonstrative, and want to prove that they are reliable.

Level 5 is where type Two's helpfulness starts to become intrusive. At this point, the Two starts sending mixed signals because their generosity comes with expectations. They need to be needed, which causes them to meddle and "control" in the name of love.

Level 6 is where a type thinks too highly of their giving nature and seems to wear an air of self-importance and self-righteousness. They are also quite needy, presumptuous, and condescending. As we start to see the decline of that healthy giving nature, this type two is more of a martyr than anything else, and they demand that others praise and acknowledge everything they do.

Unhealthy levels

Level 7 sees a turn to the dark side of type two, where that nurturing and relationship-building ability is used as a tool for manipulation and deception. This person isn't shy of using guilt and shaming tactics to get what they want. They start belittling those around them and using disparaging words. They've also lost touch with their emotions. Instead of tending to their needs, this type Two turns to food and medication as coping mechanisms. The sympathy they get for their problems is hugely pleasing, and it's where we find some keeping themselves permanently in this state as a way of getting attention and love from others.

Level 8 is a Two that's very domineering and coercive. All they want is to "get their way," They possess a strong sense of entitlement, feeling that people owe them something for being such givers.

Level 9 is the most undeveloped stage of development for type Two, and they thrive in victim mentality. They see themselves as taken advantage of, turning them into angry, resentful, bitter, and aggressive individuals. That usually leads to chronic health problems.

Addictions:

To cope with and suppress some of the emotional and psychological unrest that this type faces, especially at the unhealthy levels of development, Twos may resort to over-the-counter meds and binge eating. The overeating or "stress eating" comes from this need to fill the void or lack of love they are experiencing.

HOW TO RECOGNIZE IF YOU'RE AN ENNEAGRAM TWO

Let's look at some easy-to-spot traits for an Enneagram type Two, and make sure you take note of how many you identify with. Bear in mind that some of these traits will be more pronounced in healthy Twos while others will be more present in unhealthy Twos.

- You're strongly driven to create meaningful relationships with others, and you enjoy making people feel valued and important.
- Strangers tend to walk up to you and ask for directions or help. All your friends and family find it easy to ask you for advice or discuss personal matters because you feel warm and understanding.
- You're highly attuned to the needs of others and can quickly tell how someone feels even if they don't tell you.
- Your communication style is warm, loving, compassionate, and empathetic.
- You invest a lot of time staying in touch with the people in your world. Relationships are what you value most.
- When it comes to your romantic relationships, you enjoy playing a more supportive role, and you tend to be the more affectionate and affirming one in the relationship.
- You're attentive, engaged, and present when interacting with others which can sometimes become overwhelming, especially when they are being dramatic.
- You don't like criticism or competition.
- At your best, you feel creative, comfortable in your skin, and accepting of who you are.

- Sometimes, you worry that having needs and expressing them to another is wrong. Your fear of being selfish is prevalent, and that can sometimes cause you to neglect your own needs or even say "no" to things you don't enjoy.

STRUGGLES THAT TYPE TWOS MIGHT HAVE

Saying "No."

Selfishness is a big deal to a type Two, and the last thing she wants to do is come across as such, so she never says no. It's hard for a generous giving type Two to say no even when she knows it's the right thing to do. Most of the time, a Two just over-extends herself because she doesn't want to appear unreliable or unhelpful. Because the self-worth and personal value of a type Two are centered on being good and giving generously, she often has a terrible time balancing the demands of others and tending to her own needs, which leads me to my next point.

Taking care of your needs

Type Twos are notoriously good at self-neglect, all in the name of serving others. Their self-sacrificing nature can often create many internal issues because they never have time to tend to their own emotional, spiritual, or physical needs. This is especially true for average and unhealthy Twos who are constantly battling between wanting to help themselves and helping others so they can continue to receive love.

Feeling unloved

Average and unhealthy Twos fear that they're unlovable, and so they do everything possible to serve others in return for that love they crave. It's not uncommon for a type Two to feel empty, unseen, misunderstood, or even underappreciated, but that's usually because they "overdo" things purely expecting to receive the same generosity back.

GROWTH TIPS FOR TWOS

#1: Set healthy boundaries

Saying No is hard, I know, but unless you start creating healthy boundaries for yourself, you'll end up resenting the very people you're trying to help. Remind yourself that it's okay to say "No, I can't do that right now" or No, [fill in the blank]. Start with small things that feel less selfish and work your way up. And whenever you feel like someone is just trying to take advantage of you, have the courage to speak up and let them know you won't do it because they don't feel genuine. Don't be afraid to use your words and express your feelings. Trust me, those that truly love you don't want you to be a doormat.

#2: Prioritize self-care

What are some things you can do to make yourself feel special? Take a special and long bath each week, sign up for a painting class just for the fun of it or treat yourself to weekly massages at the spa. Anything you can do to take care of yourself, including getting proper sleep, eating healthy, making time for exercise, and more, are all ways to practice self-care. This is not selfish; it's how you fill yourself fully so you can have the energy to generously give and take care of others.

#3: Practice self-love, self-acceptance, and compassion

Self-love and compassion are essential for all enneagram types, but it's paramount for you because your type tends to completely forget that you have needs, too. Average and unhealthy levels of development will require a lot more work because anger is strong at these lower levels, but you can learn to love, accept and heal yourself. There are many spiritual teachers who are great teaching strategies for self-love, including Louise Hay and Deepak Chopra. Find a spiritual teacher that resonates and implement the self-love practices they offer. Be patient with yourself as you go through these practices, and no matter what, don't quit on yourself.

#4: Affirm yourself

Consider leaving yourself little notes all over the house with statements that make you feel good about yourself. For example, "I am loved," "I am loveable," "I love and approve of myself," or "I am beautiful, and everyone loves and accepts me for who I am."

#5: Carve out some "alone time" as often as possible.

I would encourage you to make this a daily practice even if you're alone for half an hour. It's better than nothing. While alone, do some "check-ins" to see how you're feeling, what you're thinking and which needs are unmet. Regularly taking time out to be with your thoughts and emotions will ensure you avoid the trap of thinking your source of joy or love comes from others.

TYPE 3: THE ACHIEVER/ PERFORMER

Overview of type Three:

Type Threes are called competitive achievers because they love being the best and having the best in life. Threes are hardworking, often image-conscious, goal-oriented, and have an inner drive that's almost unstoppable. Their charisma and impressive outer appearance make them very appealing, and that makes an excellent first impression. People tend to like Threes a lot because they possess a lot of remarkable accomplishments and social niceties. They are energetic doers and eager to produce things that cause them to feel and be perceived as significant.

At work, they will come across as principled, resourceful, driven, motivated, and encouraging to others, especially when everyone is moving toward a shared goal.

Different types of Threes will view the world based on their level of development, but as a general rule of thumb, healthy Threes are authentic, self-accepting, and make great role models. Average Threes are overly concerned with their image and what others think of them. They typically struggle with workaholism and "busyness." Unhealthy Threes are excessively competitive, dismissive, and hard to deal with. Their entire self-worth and self-identity are tied to their possessions and accomplishments.

Within the Centers of Intelligence triad, type Threes fall into the "heart" center where shame is the core emotion to resolve.

A healthy type Three will come across as ambitious, courageous, confident, charismatic, optimistic, hardworking, adaptable, inspiring, and success-oriented. These are actually pretty distinct qualities that one would easily observe in type Threes.

At their best, Threes are great role models, the best in their fields, and excellent at inspiring others to unlock their potential.

Core Desire: Threes most desire to feel worthwhile and valuable.

Core Fear: Threes struggle with the fear of being worthless and failing. The fear of being insignificant drives this type to find ways to be successful and influential.

What motivates a type Three? Attention and admiration are the biggest motivators for this personality type. Their need to be significant and impressive causes them to stretch and do more and go the extra mile.

Wings:

Type Three has the Two-Wing, which is "The Charmer," and the Four-Wing, which is "The Professional."

Arrows and their meaning:

The type has two arrows, namely 6 and 9. When moving in the direction of disintegration and stress (nine), Threes are vain, disengaged, and apathetic. However, the arrow pointing to growth and integration (six) shows us that deceitful, competitive Threes can transform into collaborative and service-oriented individuals like healthy Sixes.

Examples of famous people:

Some well-known people sharing the Enneagram type Two include Bill Clinton, Arnold Schwarzenegger, Muhammed Ali, Andy Warhol, Oprah Winfrey, Deepak Chopra, Tony Robbins, Madonna, Sting, Will Smith, Whitney Houston, Lady Gaga, Brooke Shields, Tiger Woods, Elvis Presley, Jamie Foxx, Richard Gere, Cat Deeley, Anne Hathaway, and Reese Whitherspoon.

Type Three levels of development:

There are different expressions of type Threes that you'll need to learn. At various stages of development, a type Three will exhibit certain behavior and attitudes depending on how disconnected they are from their higher Self. Let's look at each level.

Healthy levels

Level 1 is a type Three at their best. This individual is self-accepting, authentic, charitable, humble, gentle, benevolent, and excellent at unlocking greatness in themselves and others.

Level 2 is where a Three is energetic, competent, self-assured, and believes in their own value. Their charming and gracious desirable nature draws people to them.

Level 3 is where type Three is pretty grounded in certain admirable cultural qualities depending on what they were conditioned into. If the person grew up in a family that values success in the form of fame, they would work to become a famous actor, model, writer, or some kind of public figure. Those that are from a religious family might become some kind of religious figure or somebody noteworthy who is admired by their community. At this level, type Three is ambitious and eager to prove themselves as the best.

Average levels

Level 4 is where we start to see a somewhat negating shade forming. Type three is highly concerned with performance, doing their job well, and getting credit for their work. They have a strong need to achieve goals, and their self-worth is tied to their accomplishments. This type Three is terrified of failure, and they constantly compare themselves with others in search of status and success. Nothing matters more than climbing as high as they can in their career and society so others can see they are the best.

Level 5 is where average Threes get too consumed by their social status and public image. They work hard to have the right "package" according to the expectations of others. While they are still very efficient and pragmatic, they've started losing touch with their emotions and true identity. To save their public image, they can sometimes do some questionable things. Intimacy at this level of development is very poor as they struggle to have real connections. Everything is staged and phony.

Level 6 is where type Three feels superior to others while also struggling with inferiority when dealing with those they consider more successful. They are pretty narcissistic and have inflated notions about their talents and accomplishments. Some even embellish information about themselves so they can appear more impressive. When dealing with people they feel are less competent, they can be pretty dismissive and condescending. Jealousy and contempt for the more successful start to take root at this point.

Unhealthy levels

Level 7 sees a turn to the dark side for type Three as they become opportunistic, exploitative, and jealous. They are willing to do "whatever it takes" to preserve the illusion of their superiority and struggle deeply with the fear of failure.

Level 8 is where a type Three really turns devious, malicious, and untrustworthy. At this point, the individual will betray their friends, sabotage other people's success, and "elbow" their way to the top. They've become petty and overly competitive about everything. Anyone who is doing better than them is now perceived as a threat, and their jealousy is now taking a toll on their judgment.

Level 9 is where a type Three goes full-on evil, turning into a vindictive, ruthless, obsessive person destroying whatever stands in their way, especially when they perceive that thing or person as a threat. This type Three exhibits psychopathic behavior, and their energy is completely misdirected, making them quite dangerous to their own well-being and that of others. Most people who have narcissistic personality disorder fall into this category.

Addictions:

To cope with and suppress some of the emotional and psycholog-ical unrest that this type faces, especially at the unhealthy levels of development, Threes may resort to excessive intake of stimu-lants, cocaine, steroids or partake in radical surgery for cosmetic improvement. They might also work themselves to exhaustion trying to prove themselves to the world.

HOW TO RECOGNIZE IF YOU'RE AN ENNEAGRAM THREE

Let's look at some easy-to-spot traits for an Enneagram type Three and take note of how many you identify with. Bear in mind that some of these traits will be more pronounced in healthy Threes while others will be more identifiable with unhealthy Threes.

- Your internal drive and entire DNA is set on productivity. You seem to have this innate desire and sense of urgency to do more in life. Where Enneagrams pursue "work-life balance" and peace through rest of relationships, you're running in the opposite direction. Peace of mind for you is knowing that you're building something magnificent.
- You tend to be overly competitive even when it's unnecessary, especially at those lower levels of development.
- There's an inherent gift of being able to read a room and change your persona accordingly. Some call it shapeshifting and think of it as something evil; you disagree, of course.
- You're poised, charismatic, and intuitively know what to say in almost any situation. You can make friends and create allies out of just about anyone.

- Your image matters to you greatly, and you enjoy accentuating your best features.
- You consistently think about the future and how it could be better. Many would call that being a visionary, and you agree!
- You struggle with insecurities and feelings of emptiness, especially at those average and unhealthy levels of development. That often causes you to cover up and "mask" those weaknesses, so you can still appear impressive.

STRUGGLES THAT TYPE THREES MIGHT HAVE

Having to put up with inefficiency and incompetence

Threes are naturally hard-working individuals who believe in developing their talents and skills. Nothing is more insulting than incompetence, so when they have to work with lazy, disorganized, or inefficient people, it's simply unbearable. It's crazy to a type Three that people can be so unfocused and easily distracted by trivial things. Working with these "regular" people is quite a struggle.

Inferiority superiority complex

This is more pronounced at average and unhealthy levels of development when a Three is very prone to comparing themselves with others. When surrounded by people less successful, the Three feels very proud and superior. On the other hand, when surrounded by more successful people, the Three experiences an overwhelming sense of insecurity and inferiority. Overcoming this struggle takes a lot of deep personal development work and self-discovery so that a Three can finally become content with who they are and what they've accomplished.

Feeling unloved

Many Threes feel that others love them because of their accomplishments and outer success. Sometimes, they struggle to practice self-love because of this very thing. Without your public image, special status, and achievements, do you know who you are? Would you still feel worthy and loveable if it was all taken away? That underlying fear that your self-worth is tied to what you do and what you have is the main reason you get fixated on competing and winning at all costs. Somewhere along with your development, you were conditioned to believe that in order to survive, your focus should be on performance and action. And while there's nothing wrong with excellence and performance, it should never be the measure of your value.

Burnout

Type Threes are obsessively focused on success and achievement. That often tunes them out of their physiological and psychological needs. Over time, they struggle with fatigue, sleep deprivation, and other health issues, all in the name of chasing after that dream. If any or all of the above sounds familiar, it's time to take control of your health. Take care of your mind and body if you want to accomplish more in life. Use the technology at hand to set timers that enable you to pause during the day and hydrate or even power nap. Do you need to work long hours? That's okay. Just make sure you eat well, exercise, drink plenty of water, avoid too much caffeine and as soon as you can get a break, take some vacation time to reset. You can also learn some of the techniques and practices shared at the end of the book so you can integrate some healthy rituals into your hectic lifestyle. No one is asking you to stop being who you are. Living the Enneagram isn't about giving up your dreams but pursuing worthwhile desires in a holistic way that positively serves you and everyone else.

GROWTH TIPS FOR THREES

#1: Ground yourself worth and value in something more than accomplishments

Although you're very success-oriented and value accomplishments, realize that nothing you do adds or detracts from your true self-worth. That will be a hard concept to grasp at first, but the more you discover your true self, the easier it will be to shift your anchor from earthly, transient things to a higher, indestructible Source. That will bring you a newfound sense of security, joy, and confidence to keep developing and accomplishing in life but with less egotism.

#2: Prioritise rest and downtime

It's common for a Three to work themselves to the ground. That's neither healthy nor necessary. To accomplish greatness in your life and have the lasting influence and legacy you dream of, rest, relaxation, downtime, and you should also prioritize family time. Make an effort to slow down regularly and enjoy the present moment. It doesn't have to interfere with your work if you get creative about this. For example, you could choose to make Friday mornings a time for connecting with people, calling up friends, having breakfast with family, doing some yoga, pilates, or some other form of relaxing, enjoyable activity. Find what routine aligns with your lifestyle and schedule, and then stick to it.

#3: Cultivate empathy and compassion

It's easy to get sucked into "doing" mode and forget that people skills are an essential factor for long-term success. Emotional talk and empathy don't come naturally for many Threes, so you might need to work on this. Have enough self-awareness to recognize how good or bad you are at showing compassion when interacting with someone. Catch yourself when you respond to someone's pain or complaint without empathy. There are plenty of small things you can do to increase these qualities where lacking. A good starting point is to practice mindfulness. We'll talk more about this in the last section of the book.

#4: Choose to be your authentic self instead of what the world expects you to be

A common belief among Threes is that the world only cares about winners. The limitations of such thinking need to be addressed, especially if you lack enough self-awareness to maintain your authentic self even as you pursue success. It's important to refocus your energy on becoming the best version of yourself instead of competing to beat others or impress them in any way. Will Smith has a great statement that goes something like this: "We spend money that we do not have on things we do not need to impress people who do not care." There's no upside to that kind of approach, so it's best to focus on unleashing your best self rather than impressing a world that doesn't really care.

CHAPTER 6

ENNEAGRAM PERSONALITY TYPING SYSTEM PART 2

TYPE 4: THE INDIVIDUALIST/ ROMANTIC

Overview of type Four:

Type Fours are commonly called individualists because they are very self-focused and view themselves as unique and "different" from everyone else. They are passionate (sometimes over-emotional) and often moody. Many of the best artists and performers identify with this enneagram type.

The people who identify as type Four tend to be highly self-aware, sensitive, and often very creative, or at least very unafraid to express their creativity. As non-conformist and repelled by social status, individualists like to stand out and show the world how different they are either through their fashion choices or their unconventional lifestyles and creative output. They spend a significant portion of their lives reflecting on the past and ever seeking to discover their true identity. As such, every experience and feeling is considered valuable as though it offers a clue to some deeper meaning about life and themselves. This self-reflection can sometimes become dangerous, especially if the individual over identifies as being more flawed in some way than others. More than any other group, type Fours have difficulty detaching from what they consider personal inadequacies and deficiencies. They swing between feelings of true "aristocracy" and deep feelings of shame and fears that they are somehow deeply flawed. Fours are emotionally complex, to say the least. At work, they tend to fluctuate, sometimes being warm, compassionate, and emotional, while other times, they can be totally dry and cold. There's often an underlying tone of sadness in their communication, even when they've done good work.

Different types of Fours will view the world based on their level of development. Still, as a general rule of thumb, healthy Fours are compassionate, self-aware. They've found a way to live with and integrate both joy and suffering. Unhealthy Fours are trapped in a torture chamber of their own making and suffer from self-victimization, envy, and hopelessness. That makes them highly destructive.

Within the Centers of Intelligence triad, type Fours fall into the "heart" center alongside type Twos and Threes. In greater degrees than types Two and Three, the type Fours are more likely to fully embrace feelings of grief and sadness. Feelings of shame are more pronounced and expressed in this type as well. They really do have a hard time believing that they can be loved for who they are. Although they are in tune with their emotions, it's a very complex relationship and not always healthy.

Some descriptive qualities you might recognize in type Four include self-awareness, melancholy, expressive, idealistic, creativity, and emotional sensitivity.

At their best, Fours are compassionate, creative, and open-hearted. They seek meaning and depth in everything they do and constantly strive for personal discovery and creative expression.

Core Desire: Fours long to feel significant, be unique, and find their true identity. They also long to experience the same happiness they sometimes see in others.

Core Fear: There's a profound and piercing sense of missing out on happiness and connection that eats away at Fours. It's further amplified by the fact that they feel different and unique, which means they don't think anyone can truly get them or see their genuine magnificence.

What motivates a type Four? All Fours, to varying degrees, want to express their creativity and individuality. They are driven by this need to create and surround themselves with beauty (however, one may define beauty depending on their level of development).

Wings:

Type Four has the Three-Wing, which is "The Aristocrat," and the Five-Wing, which is "The Bohemian."

Arrows and their meaning:

Type Four has two connecting arrows, namely 2 and 1. When moving in the direction of disintegration and stress (two), aloof Fours become over-involved and clingy like an unhealthy Two. However, the arrow pointing to growth and integration (one) shows an envious, emotionally turbulent Four transforming into a more conscientious and objective individual like a healthy One.

Examples of famous people:

Some well-known people sharing the Enneagram type Four include Pyotr I. Tchaikovsky, Virginia Woolf, Miles Davis, Bob

Dylan, Paul Simon, Rumi, Frédéric Chopin, Alanis Morrisette, Jonny Depp, Nicolas Cage, Cher, and Gustav Mahler.

Type Four levels of development:

There are different expressions of type Four that you'll need to learn. At various stages of development, a type Four will exhibit certain behavior and attitudes depending on how disconnected they are from their higher Self. Let's look at each level.

Healthy levels

Level 1 is when a type Four is at their best. They are incredibly creative, expressing both the personal and universal connection. Most of the time, this will be in a work of art. This type Four is inspired. They've found that inner emotional balance and have adequately understood their identity. That makes them self renewing, regenerating, and almost whimsical as they are able to make every moment seem magical. Every experience is naturally transformed into something meaningful for them and those around them.

Level 2 is where type Four expresses their compassion and gentle nature. This Four is keenly aware of their inner impulses and become sensitive to his or her feelings and intuition. They are introspective, highly self-aware, and spend most of their time alone searching for self.

Level 3 is when we see a type Four really fighting for that sense of uniqueness and individuality. They are emotionally honest, self-revealing, humane, and unafraid to show their vulnerability. Their perspective on life and who they are is quite ironic, and they have an uncanny way of being serious and funny all at once.

Average levels

Level 4 is where a type Fours holds a romantic orientation to life, and their main focus is creating beautiful aesthetic environments that promote certain inner moods. They are very in touch with their imagination and possess a heightened reality founded on fantasy and passion.

Level 5 is where we see a more self-absorbed and introverted Four. At this point, the individual is very moody, hypersensitive, overly self-conscious, and often withdraws from the public eye to protect their self-image. This Four takes everything personally and can be really hard to deal with at work. The reason is that it's better to be isolated while they try to figure out their turbulent inner world.

Level 6 is where introspection starts to create shadows that haunt the individual. A Four at this level feels that they are different from everyone else and lack access to the joys everyone else seems to have. This individual becomes very melancholic and often falls back into a self-created fantasy world where they feel safer. They use a lot of self-pity and already start showing signs of envy. Not much gets done from this point on because it's hard to be productive when one is giving up on living.

Unhealthy levels

Level 7 is where type Four takes a downward spiral into the dark side of their personality. A Four at this level is chronically envious of others, ashamed, emotionally paralyzed, depressed, and angry at themselves because none of their dreams are materializing. This drains them of all their energy, making them super unproductive.

Level 8 is where the torment starts for a Four. Delusion, self-contempt, self-loathing, and blame take center stage. When they are not hating themselves, they are busy blaming others for their torture-filled existence.

Level 9 is where a Four hits rock bottom and is most disconnected from their higher self. At this point, the individual feels hopeless, powerless, and incapable of becoming anything more than what they are now. That makes them highly self-destructive and extreme. Some use alcohol and drugs to escape this life of torment, and others consider suicide. This is a hazardous level for type Four, and getting immediate help is advised.

Addictions:

To cope with the emotional and psychological turmoil this type faces, especially at those unhealthy levels of development, Fours may resort to alcohol, tobacco, prescription drugs, heroin, or even cosmetic surgery depending on their thought process and what they are attempting to erase from their lives.

HOW TO RECOGNIZE IF YOU'RE AN ENNEAGRAM FOUR

Let's look at some easy-to-spot traits for an Enneagram type Four and take note of how many you identify with. Bear in mind that some of these traits will be more pronounced in healthy Fours while others will be more identifiable with unhealthy Fours.

- You're highly attuned to your emotions and sensitive to other people and their feelings.
- It's easy for your to form deep connections with people.
- You're imaginative, creative, and a deep thinker.
- Authenticity and vulnerability are words that best describe you when interacting with the world.
- You like to express yourself through dance, writing, music, poetry, or other creative expressions.

STRUGGLES THAT TYPE FOURS MIGHT HAVE

Using pain as fuel for creativity

Fours are notorious for chasing after pain and sadness to fuel their creativity among the heart-centered types. If you're a Four, have you found yourself doing that at any point? Most Fours believe that art or originality is only achieved through intense emotion (usually negative emotion). Do you? If so, that will keep you stuck in a sea of negativity. Contrary to popular belief among the Fours, you don't have to be in pain to create something precious for the world.

Melancholy

In stressful situations, almost all Fours struggle with feelings of melancholy which quickly leads to self-pity and depression for the unhealthy type Fours.

Feeling misunderstood

Fours often feel misunderstood by other people. It might be that others are simply confused by the Four's ever-changing mood or that they just aren't used to dealing with a person who openly shares their most vulnerable and painful emotion. Whatever the case might be, if you're a Four and feel that people don't appreciate or understand you enough, instead of doing what unhealthy Fours would do, i.e., withdraw from the world, choose to figure out a way to connect with others in a way that develops both you and them.

Envy

Many Fours (especially those at average and unhealthy levels) struggle with deep feelings of envy because they see in others what they feel is missing in them, which stirs up jealousy. If you often compare yourself to others and feel less about your own life, this should be addressed in healthy ways.

GROWTH TIPS FOR FOURS

#1: Watch your self-talk

Inner dialogue can either be negative or positive. It tends to be negative for many of us, which can poison confidence and self-esteem. In the case of type Four, negative self-talk can be detrimental, even destructive.

Pay close attention to that inner critic and determine to retrain that inner voice into a more loving, kinder, and positively affirming voice. This will require effort and practice on your end, so start small. Whenever you catch yourself thinking ill about yourself or another, pause, take a few breaths and tell yourself, "Here I go again. Throwing myself down the pit of despair. Well, not this time. I choose to think a different thought."

Proceed to find the next best thought that is more positive than your previous negative thought.

#2: Don't believe every thought and feeling you have

Many Fours become slaves to their minds and assume the role of victim when negative, overwhelming thoughts and emotions kick in. Here's the thing, no matter how tormenting a thought is, it's just a thought. You can choose to think a different thought. Just because the idea came to you doesn't mean it should take residence in your mental home. For example, if you feel envious and think evil thoughts, you can refuse to hold on to that emotion. You could cast it away from your mind and body immediately and command it to stay away from your mental home. With your imagination, open the door of your mental home, command that thought or emotion to get out, and lock the door! Try it next time an unpleasant feeling shows up.

#3: Practice self-discipline

Given the tendency to be passive and even procrastinate, I'm encouraging you to develop healthy routines that enable you to practice self-discipline.

Everything should have its time and place, e.g., a time to just wander with your imagination and a time to be objective, pragmatic and productive. The key here is to build a healthy routine you enjoy and then stick with it. By developing your own personalized routine, not only are you exercising your power of individuality, but you're also giving yourself rules of engagement that foster the best quality of life possible.

#4: Find common ground between you and others

The only way to eliminate that horrid feeling of being "different" from others is to train yourself to find common ground while socializing with people. The more things you can find in common, the easier it will be to create connections with others and find the people who love and accept you for who you are.

#5: Celebrate your wins no matter how small

One way to avoid the trap of shame and inadequacy is to notice the things you're doing well and the strengths you possess. Whenever you set a goal and achieve it, celebrate that, no matter how small. If you have a work or health goal, create mini-milestones that will keep you accountable and also help you know when to celebrate yourself.

TYPE 5: THE INVESTIGATOR

Overview of type Five:

Type Fives are also called observers or quiet specialists because they are driven by the desire to gain knowledge and understanding. They are sober-minded, disciplined, and highly intelligent. Fives are most comfortable in the realm of thought where they can think, investigate, discover and objectively solve complex problems. They care a lot about finding out why things are the way they are and how the world works, whether it's the local environment, the planet, or the cosmos. While many type Fives are scientifically oriented, some are drawn to humanities and arts. In fact, it's not uncommon for a Five to be artistically inclined even if they pursue a scientific discipline.

Fives spend a lot of time curiously observing and contemplating everything around them to gain new knowledge. They don't care much about what's already familiar and established in society. Instead, they want to be on the leading edge of that new idea or discovery. A Five's attention is usually attracted to the unusual, the overlooked, the bizarre, or the unknown territory. Gaining knowledge that others don't have is thrilling for a type Five. That's why many of them choose to specialize in areas where they can get enough expertise to be considered an authority in that subject. At work, Fives are private, prefer to work autonomously, and tend to analytically approach each project or subject. You may notice they don't like small talk and generally refrain from social interaction unless it's a topic they have an intense interest in.

Different types of Fives will view the world based on their level of development, but as a general rule of thumb, healthy Fives are self-reliant, confident, influential pioneers who are great at dealing with emergencies or crises because they know how to remain calm and objectively analyze the situation at hand. Unhealthy Fives are withdrawn from society, radical, and lacking emotional awareness. They struggle to understand their own emotions and quickly develop tunnel vision, making it hard to have healthy relationships.

Within the Centers of Intelligence triad, type Fives fall into the "head" center alongside type Sixes and Sevens. The underlying unresolved emotion for the thinkers is fear. Fives attempt to avoid the feeling of fear and anxiety by withdrawing and protecting their inner resources.

Some descriptive qualities you might recognize in type Five include curiosity, scholarly, perceptivity, autonomy, insightful and private.

At their best, Fives are curious visionary pioneers who tend to be ahead of their time. They have incredible foresight and a calm demeanor that brings great comfort to others.

Core Desire: To be self-sufficient, free, and knowledgeable. Fives want to understand why things work as they do, and most desire to be competent and feel secure in their knowledge and inner resources.

Core Fear: Type Fives fear being incapable or helpless.

What motivates a type Five? All type Fives to varying degrees and depending on how healthy their development is long to under-stand their environment. They are inspired by their curiosity and desire to know and understand as much as possible.

Wings:

Type Five has the Four-Wing, which is "The Iconoclast," and the Six-Wing, which is "The Problem Solver."

Arrows and their meaning:

Type Five has two connecting arrows, namely 7 and 8. When moving in the direction of disintegration and stress (seven), detached Fives become scattered, absent-minded and hyperactive like an unhealthy Seven. However, the arrow pointing to growth and integration (eight) shows a detached Five transforming into a more confident and decisive individual like a healthy Eight.

Examples of famous people:

Some well-known people sharing the enneagram type Five include Albert Einstein, Stephen Hawkin, Friedrich Nietzsche, Stephen King, Siddhartha Gautama Buddha, Eckhart Tolle, Emily Dickinson, Bill Gates, Mark Zuckerberg, Jane Goodall, Jodie Foster, and Angela Merkel.

Type Five levels of development:

There are different expressions of type Five that you'll need to learn. At various stages of development, a type Five will exhibit certain behavior and attitudes depending on how disconnected they are from their higher Self. Let's look at each level.

Healthy levels

Level 1 is a type Five at their best and highest development. At this level, the individual is open-minded, engaged, and sees the world as whole and abundant. This Five sees large complex issues with clarity and precision. That leads them to pioneer discoveries and find entirely new ways of doing and perceiving things. They have also learned to acknowledge, process, and even embrace their emotional side, making them well-rounded and powerful human beings.

Level 2 is where type Five is intensely focused on their object of attention. They are extraordinarily perceptive and curious about whatever they study, preferring to invest most of their time in observation mode.

Level 3 is where a Five invests all their time to become an expert in a specific field. They are innovative, highly independent, and produce precious works. Knowledge thrills and excites them.

Average levels

Level 4 is where a Five spends most of their time thinking things through and building mental models and visuals to figure things out. At this point of development, the individual is slow to take action on their ideas because they prefer to gather as many resources as possible, prepare and test out their ideas in their head first.

Most people tend to be fascinated by off-beat esoteric subjects, even those involving dark and disturbing elements. They are intense and high-strung and spend most of their time alone. Level 5 is the point at which a type Five typically starts showing significant signs of detachment.

Level 6 is where type Five takes an antagonistic stance toward anything that threatens their inner world or personal vision. They are cynical, argumentative, and hold incredibly radical views on life.

Unhealthy levels

Level 7 is where we see a downward spiral into the dark side of the personality. This type Five is isolated from reality, eccentric and nihilistic. Their fear is beginning to take center stage, causing them to be very unstable and detached from everything and everyone.

Level 8 is where a Five becomes obsessed and frightened by their own thoughts. Threatening ideas overwhelm them, and they turn into horrific delirious individuals suffering from phobias and reality distortions. At this point, many develop poor eating and sleeping habits and even neglect their hygiene.

Level 9 is the rock bottom for type Five, and they become highly susceptible to suicide. Some people have a psychotic breakdown, and others become deranged, self-destructive, and entirely out of touch with their emotions.

Addictions:

To cope with the emotional and psychological turmoil this type faces, especially at those unhealthy levels of development, Fives may resort to psychotropic drugs for mental stimulation and escape. Some may use narcotics to deal with their anxiety.

HOW TO RECOGNIZE IF YOU'RE AN ENNEAGRAM FIVE

Let's look at some easy-to-spot traits for an Enneagram type Five and take note of how many you identify with. Bear in mind that some of these traits will be more pronounced in healthy Fours while others will be more identifiable with unhealthy Fives.

- Others often say you come across as emotionally disconnected, aloof, over-analytical, and distant. Maybe your romantic partner complains about some of these traits?
- You're not big on small talk, but you enjoy deep conversations around your topics of interest.
- Privacy is critical to you and non-negotiable. It's one of the reasons you're not a fan of social media.
- Being self-sufficient, independent, and having complete autonomy over your life are also non-negotiable.
- You're a minimalist.

- It feels like the world is very intrusive and draining. Hence, you do your best to create firm boundaries to protect your energy and resources.
- You like to hoard knowledge, space, and even time alone.
- You're not into large crowds, big gatherings, or many friends. Your relationships are few but very strong.
- Curiosity is one of the key qualities you recognize about yourself. There's an unquenchable thirst for knowledge and figuring things out.

STRUGGLES THAT AN ENNEAGRAM FIVE MIGHT FACE

Getting stuck in your head

There's a common statement you might have heard several times in your lifetime, especially if you are a type Five. "Get out of your head ." Let's face it, Fives spend a lot of time lost in their heads. While it is nice to dissect everything and everyone around you or to create internal models of the world, over time, this will create a deep struggle as the gap between your inner mental world and this outer objective world widens. A healthy Five learns to integrate both worlds and spend healthy amounts of time swimming in their ocean of thoughts and mental constructs without neglecting the objective world.

Underlying insecurity

In the book "Personality Types: Using the Enneagram for Self Discovery, Don Riso and Russ Hudson state that type Fives "usually try to avoid getting deeply involved with others because people are unpredictable and potentially demanding. The average and unhealthy levels of development struggle the most with this thought because they believe there's always a catch. This is a form of insecurity often masked with a detached, carefree demeanor.

You might think that you don't care about others, but the under-lying issue is that you fear you won't be competent enough to handle any unpredictable challenges that arise from engaging with others. That's something that needs to be resolved.

Distractions

Whether you're a healthy, average, or unhealthy Five, you'll appreciate the mention of distractions because that's a universal struggle for all Fives. Everyone who identifies as a type Five hates being interrupted or forced to deal with the noisy outside world. Technology is fantastic for a knowledge thirsty Five. But it can also be a source of anguish, especially if you have family and friends who keep nagging you offline and online. When there's a lot of noise, obligations, and too frequent interactions, it feels as though people don't respect your privacy and personality. Instead of suffering in silence or, worse still, shutting yourself away from people, consider speaking up and letting others know that you need quiet, uninterrupted time. If apps tend to irritate you, create a structure that enables you to enjoy them when convenient and shut them out when you need peace and quiet. Find healthy ways to protect your personal space without isolating yourself.

Connecting with your emotions

The thinker in your struggles to reconcile the value of emotions thus ensues the constant rift between reason and feeling. It's easy to detach from your feelings, block them out and hope they will disappear. What you need to realize is that your emotions serve a higher purpose. They are just as important to your growth and fulfillment as your intellect. Your ideas and execution ability will exponentially grow when you harmoniously integrate both thought and emotion.

Not having enough alone time

It's good to find a healthy balance between being alone and connecting with others. If you're a Five, you know that you need more alone time than most people. That can create friction within relationships, especially if you have to deal with someone extroverted. Forcing yourself to be around people isn't healthy for your development. Still, neither is detaching too much from the world of people.

GROWTH TIPS FOR FIVES

#1: Let the world in

Okay, maybe not the whole world but know that it's okay to step out of your comfort zone and trust people. The universe is benevolent. It's okay to have relationships, trust others and even share your feelings. I know it will take practice, so start small. One good friend at a time is all you need to get started.

#2: Invest time daily to connect with your body and emotions

While it is lovely to spend most of your time in your mind, it's even more powerful to consciously create that mind-body connection. Consider experimenting with different exercises and activities that link your emotions, body, and mind. Find something you enjoy: painting, playing an instrument, creative writing, journaling, yoga, or whatever else you can regularly engage in.

#3: Practice being generous with yourself

The more you can do and give to yourself, the easier it will be to perceive abundance and, in turn, give generously, whether it's your knowledge, time, or resources. Make some room for abundance in your life so you can eliminate that scary feeling of scarcity that often causes Fives to hoard things.

#4: Create a support structure that promotes your wellbeing

People who build you up and challenge you to be a better human being. Considering how obsessive and intense you can be about something you care about, I encourage you to have a support structure. Pick one or two people with whom you can absolutely share anything and everything. This can be a single individual who has access to your most disturbing thoughts emotions so they can help keep you grounded. Suppose you lose your grip on reality or get too carried away by an idea. In that case, they'll be there to bring you back into a healthy perspective so you don't lose yourself in the pursuit of knowledge. You might think it's unnecessary, but it does a lot of emotional good for both you and the one that loves you to know that you've got each other's back.

#5: Increase your self-awareness

Daily self-awareness practices will enable you to go through life mindful and more aware of how you show up and when you're starting to spiral downward in your development. Become aware when you're starting to close yourself in or when you've shut someone down. Then you can consciously take action to move in a more constructive direction.

TYPE 6: THE LOYALIST/SKEPTIC

Overview of type Six:

Type Sixes are commonly called loyalists because they are very committed to their relationships and values. Sixes are considered the most loyal, faithful, and dependable of all Enneagram types. They are also referred to as skeptics because they are often alert and trying to think several steps ahead so they can feel ready to handle worst-case scenarios. Sixes are generally incredible at troubleshooting and problem solving, but lower levels of development have Sixes who get paralyzed by this natural tendency to anticipate things going wrong. In fact, at average and unhealthy levels, a type Six is often overwhelmed by their constant worry about the future and things going wrong.

In general, Sixes are hard-working, competent, and take their time to do things the right way. While they are the most loyal, it takes time to develop that trust. But once a Six trusts you or commits themselves to something, they stick to it. They also respect rules and authority, provided they trust that source of authority and their intention. Unlike type Five, who are also thinkers, Sixes enjoy collaboration and teamwork. At work, they thrive in healthy team environments and aren't afraid to take a stand on behalf of the team's greater good despite concerns and risks. They are great at honoring commitments to people and plans and tend to approach issues with both logic and emotion. For a type Six, being prepared, safe and secure is a top priority.

Different types of Sixes will view the world based on their level of development, but as a general rule of thumb, healthy Sixes are

caring, generous, and hard-working team players who enjoy motivating colleagues and friends. They take great pride in serving their organization, developing a secure attachment style, and trusting others easily.

On the other hand, Unhealthy Sixes are highly paranoid, suspicious of everything, and paralyzed when it comes to taking action because the illusion of constant danger is too overwhelming. Unfortunately, unhealthy Sixes like to project their insecurities onto others which can cause a lot of friction in relationships.

Within the Centers of Intelligence triad, type Sixes fall into the "head" center alongside type Fives and Sevens. Within this triad, type Sixes struggle the most with their unresolved fear, and they keep swinging from trust and mistrust of the people around them and the world. The fear and anxiety in a Six can manifest in various ways, making this type the most difficult to describe and type. It also makes a Six more susceptible to mistyping their real personality. Many assume they are a type Two or a Nine.

Some descriptive qualities you might recognize in type Six include responsibility, commitment, persistence, loyal, trustworthiness, dependability, courage, attention to people, and strategy in their thinking.

At their best, Sixes are internally stable, self-reliant, trustworthy, and great team players.

Core Desire: Sixes seek security and support.

Core Fear: Losing their ground, being unprepared, and unable to defend themselves from the dangers of this world.

What motivates a type Six? Type Sixes are driven by the need to create a feeling of safety and security around them.

Wings:

Type Six has the Five-Wing, which is "The Defender," and the Seven-Wing which is "The Buddy."

Arrows and their meaning:

Type Six has two connecting arrows, namely 3 and 9. When moving in the direction of disintegration and stress (three), dutiful Sixes are arrogant and competitive like unhealthy Nines. However, the arrow pointing to growth and integration (nine) shows a fearful, pessimistic Six transforming into a more relaxed and optimistic individual like a healthy Nine.

Examples of famous people:

Some well-known people sharing the Enneagram type Six include Mike Tyson, Diana Princess of Wales, Marylin Monroe, Mel Gibson, Jennifer Aniston, Sarah Jessica Parker, Mark Twain, Woody Allen, and Eminem.

Type Six levels of development:

There are different expressions of type Six that you'll need to learn. At various stages of development, a type Four will exhibit certain behavior and attitudes depending on how disconnected they are from their higher Self. Let's look at each level.

Healthy levels

Level 1 is a type Six at their best. Here the individual is calm, trusts themselves and others, courageous, optimistic in their thinking, and makes a great leader. Their ability to affirm themselves and champion others into their greatness makes them extremely valuable in the world. This type Six has found his or her security and safety and doesn't look to external sources to provide them. They find a balance between independent and interdependent when in relation to others.

Level 2 is a type Six who is lovable, affectionate, and capable of forming permanent alliances and healthy relationships with others. Trust is essential, and they can bond quickly with others.

Level 3 is a type Six who is highly devoted to the people and things they believe in. This individual is often a great community builder. They are trustworthy, hard-working, great at troubleshooting. They bring about that cooperative spirit that glues people together, whether offline or online.

Average levels

Level 4 is a type Six not yet grounded in their own stability and safety. That means they spend most of their energy and time trying to create structures and alliances that give them that feeling of continuity and security. This individual is always on the alert and anticipating problems.

Level 5 is a type Six who struggles with anxiety and internal confusion. They keep switching from feelings of trust to mistrust, safety, and danger. This individual becomes evasive, indecisive, overly cautious, and ambivalent. They might also become a little passive-aggressive in their relationships.

Level 6 is where a Six become increasingly insecure. They turn sarcastic and blame others for their problems. At this point, their tunnel vision causes them to be very black and white, creating divisions and labeling people either as friends or enemies. This type Six loves to be authoritarian yet is highly suspicious and even fearful of authority. They find comfort in instilling fears in others as a coping mechanism to silence their own fears.

Unhealthy levels

Level 7 is where a type Six spirals downward into their dark side. Fear is pronounced in this person, and they turn panicky, volatile, and challenging to be around. They feel defenseless and desperately seek out a stronger external authority or something that can help them resolve their problems.

Level 8 is typically where the Six feels like others are out to get them. Some might even turn a little violent as they lash out and act irrationally. Ironically, their actions cause them to produce the very thing they fear.

Level 9 is the most unhealthy level for a type Six. At this point, we are dealing with a self-destructive, hysterical, and maybe even suicidal person. Most of their behavior is passive-aggressive, and they are prone to self-sabotage even the little good that they do.

Addictions:

To cope with the emotional and psychological turmoil this type faces, especially at those unhealthy levels of development, Sixes might resort to alcoholism, drug abuse, or even working excessively, all in an attempt to eliminate the dangers they perceive and fortify their security.

HOW TO RECOGNIZE IF YOU'RE AN ENNEAGRAM SIX

Let's look at some easy-to-spot traits for an Enneagram type Six and take note of how many you identify with. Bear in mind that some of these traits will be more pronounced in healthy Sixes while others will be more identifiable with unhealthy Sixes.

- You're incredibly loyal to the people you care about.
- Stability, safety, security, consistency, and predictability really matter to you.
- In some ways, you're super confident, but sometimes you're also super insecure.
- You like being direct in your communication and prefer when people are direct with you.
- You're more interested in supporting the group than being the star or having the spotlight on you.
- You value loyalty and trust in relationships.
- The desire to always do things the "right way" causes you plenty of anxiety.
- You fear being abandoned or left alone by those you trust.

- When you believe in something, you'll stick to it and will rarely change your mind no matter what.

STRUGGLES THAT AN ENNEAGRAM SIX MIGHT FACE

Pessimism and suspicion

Painting worst-case scenarios is a huge obstacle for all Sixes. While it is good to consider all angles, allowing your brain to fall into the rabbit hole of pessimism and anxiety will only do your work and health harm. Consider bringing yourself more into the present moment whenever you find yourself falling too far into skepticism.

Thinking in circles

Most unhealthy and average Sixes will find themselves thinking in circles, getting nowhere. It's easy to get stuck in a loop that breeds anxiety and fear. That's why you need to catch yourself as early as possible when your thinking starts to spiral downward and stop that momentum. Instead of overthinking things, pause and ask yourself, "what if the worst happens?" Once you answer that follow up with "and then what?" Once you answer that, keep leaning in that direction until you find yourself identifying the resources you have to handle whatever your brain tells you will go wrong. Sometimes all you need to do is show your brain that anticipating "bad things" isn't very productive and that no matter how bad your brain thinks it is, there's always a solution to every problem. Show yourself that your thinking can be brilliant enough to create constructive ideas, not just anxiety-building ones.

Phobias or counter-phobic behavior

Some Sixes avoid facing their fears and become phobic over everything as a defense mechanism. Others go to the polar extreme and put up a show of tough exterior, often putting themselves in risky situations to prove that they are fearless. This is used as a way of masking their internal uncertainty. Either way, none of these expressions are healthy, so it's best to address and resolve them in healthy ways.

GROWTH TIPS FOR SIXES

#1: Take safe risks and try new things often

Consistency and predictability are great, but they'll make you too rigid. You need to stay flexible and adaptable, so do something that regularly takes you out of your comfort zone. Start with small things like ordering a different sandwich at your favorite cafe or changing up your workout routine. The more you can show yourself that some risks are reasonable, the easier it will be to embrace change, and you might just realize that the world isn't as bad as you imagine.

#2: Cultivate self-belief

This is one of the most important things you can do to develop and improve your life. How does one increase self-belief? It starts with small, consistent steps taken daily that increase your self-esteem. Consider listening to a podcast or reading a book daily that feeds your mind with nourishing thoughts about who you are and what you're capable of. You should also set big and small goals that you move toward. As you accomplish each one (especially the mini-goals), remind yourself that it's you doing this and give yourself permission to feel good about it. Find your Truth, and you will have a solid ground to build yourself.

#3: Create daily practices and habits that help you release anxiety

Instead of spending a lot of time on your head, refocus that energy on constructive things that enable you to stay in the present moment and release stress and tension. If unsure what activities can help you with present moment awareness, check out the last section. I've shared various techniques to help you grow into a healthier version of yourself.

#4: Work on your trust meter

Trust is a big issue for you as a Six, and that means you need to give it generously if you desire to have it. That tendency to be skeptical of everything and everyone might serve you some of the time. Still, you should have it on a tight leash because, for the most part, it's easier to build healthy, lasting relationships when you're not pessimistic and skeptical. Don't be afraid to give someone your trust if it feels right, and trust in your judgment. Sure, you will come across a few mistakes here and there. The trick is to get more attuned to your inner guidance and believe that you can choose the right people to be around you.

CHAPTER 7

ENNEAGRAM PERSONALITY TYPING SYSTEM PART 3

TYPE 7: THE ENTHUSIAST

Overview of type Seven:

Type Sevens are enthusiastic pleasure-seekers because they love adventure and possess boundless energy. They are ever pursuing the next big thing that will create feelings of pleasure and happiness in their lives. Sevens are often practical with multiple talents and high-level skill sets. They are quick thinkers, creative, and able to do several things simultaneously. Their positive energy makes them highly attractive, so people really enjoy being around them. The central theme for the optimistic Seven is to plan, prepare for and seek out the next new thing because they are generally convinced that something better is just around the corner. And although their energy and personality are great for networking, promoting themselves, and their interests in the workplace, this constant restlessness can create a lot of friction. Focus doesn't come easy for a Seven, and they like to keep all their options open, so they struggle with commitment a lot. They enjoy having creative freedom and having options and flexible schedules at work. They love being around people, but it cannot be under rigid rules and structures as that will kill the spontaneity and freedom that Sevens most enjoy about interactions. Sevens thrive in environments that utilize their creative thinking and imagination. They will be the ones to explore and offer up new possibilities and future ideas. Most Sevens are extroverted and enjoy experiencing the world mainly through their physical senses.

Different types of Sevens will view the world based on their level of development. Still, as a general rule of thumb, healthy Sevens are more serene, focused, and able to concentrate their energy wisely, producing results that benefit themselves and others. They possess contagious positive energy that naturally draws in all the right opportunities and people. They can easily find that perfect work-life balance that enables them to enjoy the best of both. Unhealthy Sevens are illogical, irritable, great procrastinators, and unproductive. They struggle with responsibility and accountability and can never finish what they start. Ever jumping from one thing to the next or relationship to relationship, unhealthy Sevens aren't grounded or in control of their compulsive need for pleasure. That makes them pretty moody and emotionally unstable.

Within the Centers of Intelligence triad, type Sevens fall into the "head" center alongside type Fives and Sixes. With fear being their underlying unresolved emotion, Sevens react differently to this disconnect. They choose to do everything possible to find and sustain pleasure through their senses as their way of locking out the negative states and fear they don't wish to deal with. They seek distractions in external environments to ensure constant stimulation, which is why they are more prone than most types to fall into all kinds of addictions.

Their fear and pain avoidance are also projected onto others. You'll notice a Seven will not want to confront anyone's dark emotions, not even their own. They'd rather downplay or deny pain rather than acknowledge it. Of course, the extent to which a Seven is manifesting this denial and avoidance depends entirely on their level of development.

Some descriptive qualities you might recognize in type Sevens include curiosity, optimism, spontaneity, versatility, adventurousness, adaptability, agility, and open-mindedness.

At their best, Sevens are focused and working on worthwhile goals. They've learned to be appreciative, joyous, and satisfied with themselves and life as a whole.

Core Desire: Type Seven's most basic desire is to feel happy, satisfied, and engaged. They want to soak in all the goodness that life offers and desire to live all their lives in that pleasure.

Core Fear: The most basic fear of a Seven is that the inherent fear and negative emotions that are unresolved within them will take over and cause inescapable pain. They also fear being deprived of freedom and excitement in life, so they hate rigid rules and strict deadlines.

What motivates a type Seven? Their biggest motivation is to avoid pain, discomfort, and negativity at all costs.

Wings:

Type Seven has the Six-Wing, which is "The Entertainer," and the Eight-Wing, which is "The Realist."

Arrows and their meaning:

Type Seven has two connecting arrows, namely 1 and 5. When moving in the direction of disintegration and stress (one), scattered Sevens become critical and perfectionistic like unhealthy Ones. However, the arrow pointing to growth and integration (five) shows a scattered Seven transforming into a more focused individual like a healthy Five.

Examples of famous people:

Some well-known people sharing the enneagram Seven include Amelia Earhart, Ram Dass, John F. Kennedy, Richard Branson, Katy Perry, Elton John, The 14th Dalai Lama, Bette Midler, George Clooney, Brad Pitt, Robin Williams, Jim Carrey, Robert Downey, Jr., and Leonardo DiCaprio.

Type Seven levels of development:

There are different expressions of type Sevens that you'll need to learn. At various stages of development, a type Sevens will exhibit certain behavior and attitudes depending on how disconnected they are from their higher Self. Let's look at each level.

Healthy levels

Level 1 is a type Seven at their best. This individual lives in awe and wonder over the goodness that life offers. They assimilate experiences in-depth and experience deep appreciation and gratitude for where they are and what they have. They have accessed the joyful ecstasy of finding that much-needed spiritual alignment that provides the pleasure they were seeking externally.

Level 2 is where a Seven is most extroverted. They are cheerful, resilient, spontaneous, curious, excitable, and want to experience life to its fullest. This individual finds everything invigorating.

Level 3 is where a Seven is more of a generalist and still very invested in their multifaceted interests but in a focused way, making them highly productive. This individual accomplishes more than most and is usually great at everything they put their attention on.

Average levels

Level 4 is where a Seven starts becoming restless. They want to have more options and choices tied directly to their sense of freedom. Their sense of adventure and pleasure-seeking is more worldly as they seek external experiences and new things. This Seven is a massive consumer of the latest trends.

Level 5 is where a Seven becomes hyperactive and unable to control their compulsive need for stimulation. They are swamped and distracted doing whatever comes to mind. At this point, the fear of being bored and missing out starts to kick into high gear. They are still optimistic, witty, wisecracking, and love things that entertain them. Creative ideas continue to flow, and as they are still trying to pursue all their different interests but without a clear focus, not much is getting accomplished. They might start something or develop a great idea, but there won't be any follow-through.

Level 6 is where a Seven turn excessive in their consumption. They just can't say "no" to themselves. That causes them to become self-centered, too materialistic, and even greedy as they seek to have more and more. Nothing is ever enough for them. In terms of behavior, this Seven becomes pushy, jaded, and really demanding.

Unhealthy levels

Level 7 is where we see a downward spiral to the dark side of a Seven. At this point, the person is desperate to quell their increasing anxiety and excessive behavior. Unfortunately, they don't know how to create discipline because they've never created any structure or healthy habits, so they fall into addictions and abusive behavior. In an attempt to escape negative states of mind, they fall deeper into the dark pit of addiction.

Level 8 is where a type Seven attempts to run away from their own horrid self. Their optimism has faded, and now all that's left is never-ending anxiety and erratic mood swings.

Level 9 is the lowest level of development and definitely rock bottom for the enthusiast. At this point, the Seven has depleted all their energy and often give up on life and themselves. They quickly fall into depression and despair. Some develop dangerous and self-destructive behavior and are prone to overdosing or attempting suicide.

Addictions:

To cope with the emotional and psychological turmoil this type faces, especially at those unhealthy levels of development, Sevens might resort to all kinds of stimulants ranging from caffeine to more dangerous stuff like Cocaine. They are more likely to indulge in ecstasy pills, psychotropics, narcotics, and alcohol. Those that are into physical appearance might also take up excessive cosmetic surgery.

HOW TO RECOGNIZE IF YOU'RE AN ENNEAGRAM SEVEN

Let's look at some easy-to-spot traits for an Enneagram type Seven and take note of how many you identify with. Bear in mind that some of these traits will be more pronounced in healthy Sevens. In contrast, others will be more identifiable with unhealthy Sevens.

- You're passionately obsessed with the future and all its possibilities. In fact, you prefer focusing on the future and find the present pretty dull.

- You enjoy having lots and lots of options when it comes to just about everything. That includes your social and professional life.
- FOMO is real, and you can't stand it.
- You don't get people who say "find what you love" because you love lots of things and are pretty much multi-talented.
- "Zen" is the last word you would ever use to describe yourself.
- You have childlike enthusiasm and curiosity despite how old you are.
- People find you magnetic and say your positive energy is contagious.
- You love planning a lot. In fact, you can easily map out the next fifteen years... but two weeks from now, you'll probably have another new detailed plan.

STRUGGLES THAT AN ENNEAGRAM SEVEN MIGHT HAVE

Lack of focus

Being able to focus and concentrate is a skill that all Sevens will need to master if they want to be productive and accomplished. It's harder for average and unhealthy Sevens to concentrate and focus on a single thing long enough to see it through. If that mental fog and "out of control" feeling is getting to you, work on creating healthy routines that enable you to develop more self-discipline and focus.

Feeling constricted and trapped by routine and schedules

Since freedom is one of your core values, it's easy to feel like commitments, schedules, and other people's expectations cage you. You might desire loyal lasting relationships like marriage or long-term work contracts. Still, at the same time, these things bring you a sense of anxiety and restlessness. The key here is to reframe some of these critical commitments in your life and come to the full realization that freedom and responsibilities are not mutually exclusive.

Jack of all trades and a master of none

Most average and unhealthy Sevens will struggle to stick with something long enough to gain mastery. That can be in their professional and personal interests. Their curiosity at these lower levels of development causes them to bounce from one thing to the next. They can easily pick up new skills and abilities but quickly drop them for the next new thing. If this has been one of your struggles, the solution is to develop yourself so you can get to the point where you can pursue what you love long enough to gain real expertise.

Pain and negative emotions are your enemies

As a classic type Seven, acknowledging and processing anything that threatens that upbeat vibe is obviously going to be hard. And that's okay. Sevens are known to rationalize and justify everything that threatens their happiness because they don't want to deal with these uncomfortable emotions. If you realize this to be true of you, start catching yourself in those moments when things are bad, and you're attempting to "gloss" over or "closet" them for later. Instead, get out of your head and into your body. Become aware of those emotions and take time to explore them. Give yourself permission to experience both pleasure and pain because it enables you to become well-rounded and resilient.

GROWTH TIPS FOR SEVENS

#1: Learn to see the value of all your emotions, including the dark ones

I know this is hard if you're a Seven because you avoid all negativity and pain, including other people's. I would encourage you to keep an open mind and educate yourself a little more about the purpose these emotions serve. It will be hard to feel whole if you go through life denying certain aspects of yourself. And while dwelling in pain and negativity is not healthy, acknowledging it when it happens is ideal.

#2: Allow yourself to go deep and process all your emotions

Give yourself permission to feel all your emotions, not just the pleasant ones. The next time a negative emotion comes over you, don't run. Sit with it and take time to process it. Ask yourself, "what am I feeling, and where are you feeling it in your body?" If you can identify exactly what this negative emotion is, that will empower you to label and tame that emotion. Done well, and with much practice, this can be a liberating process.

#3: Integrate a little more discipline into your life

You might associate schedules and structure with boredom and constriction. Still, a little more discipline and self-control will actually enhance your life and aid your development. The more discipline you bring to your work and life, the more focus you'll have and the bigger the reward as you finally start seeing the results of your hard work.

#4: Slow down and be more present

I know it's fun to stay focused on the future and limitless possibilities but remember your power lies in the present moment. It's essential for you to invest more time cultivating your power in the here and now. That's the real key to further growth and progress. Check out the last chapter on practices that can enable you to become powerfully present regardless of your current level of development.

TYPE 8: THE CHALLENGER/PROTECTOR

Overview of type Eight:

Type Eights are known as challengers because they rebel against the status quo and have no problem challenging something that doesn't align with their values or take advantage of others.

Eights are powerful and strong-willed with the natural charisma and persuasive abilities that cause others to follow them into all kinds of endeavors. They are known to enjoy taking up new challenges, creating initiatives that propel change, and being in charge of everything around them. Sometimes they are also referred to as protectors because inasmuch as they like to challenge others to step out of their comfort zone, they are also very protective of the people under their care. Although Eights can come across as intimidating, aggressive, and at times argumentative, their intentions are usually in the right place because nothing is more important to them than standing up for what they believe and protecting those under their care. All Eights tend to be quite domineering, even the healthy ones. The difference is with a healthy Eight, that tendency is kept in check.

Most Eights are hard-working, self competent, pragmatic, and goal-oriented. They are often the trailblazers in our society, taking great pride in their independence and sharpness of mind. Their perception is that the world is made up of "strong" and "weak" people; they being in the "strong" category, have the responsibility of protecting the weak. One of the great passions for an Eight is to bring about justice, end oppression for and protect the vulnerable.

At work, Eights are better when they have some kind of leadership role. Most people refer to them as "bossy" because they're assertive, authoritative, and can get pretty angry when things don't go their way. They can be pretty impatient with rules and regulations and have difficulty following other people's instructions. However, they bring great energy and enthusiasm to the team. As long as things are getting done their way, everyone enjoys working with them.

Different types of Eights will view the world based on their level of development. Still, as a general rule of thumb, healthy Eights are

brave, charismatic, generous, powerful protectors who are resourceful and committed to their team or mission. They are also intensely loving and protective of their close friends and family members. Unhealthy Eights, on the other hand, are tyrannical. They are power-hungry and will destroy anything that gets in their way. Anger is a big issue for this type, and they aren't afraid to unleash it to the world, especially when they don't get what they want. In the lower levels of development, Eights can become quite vengeful and emotionally numb.

Within the Centers of Intelligence triad, type Eights fall into the "Gut" center alongside type Nines and Ones. The core unresolved emotion for this triad is anger, and Eights isn't afraid to show it. Unlike the Nines and Ones who try to repress or ignore their anger, Eights aren't shy of confrontation, issuing threats and throwing temper tantrums at a moment's notice.

Some descriptive qualities you might recognize in type Eights include brave, enthusiastic, energetic, charismatic, determined, confident, fierce, independent, self-sufficient, assertive, and protective.

At their best, Eights are inspiring, generous, and capable of achieving great things. Their self-mastery and commitment to justice and creating a good life for themselves and others strengthens and propels them into success. They are natural-born leaders, and people love following them.

Core Desire: Eights desire to have a good life and control their own destiny. They want to be the hero in their world.

Core Fear: Eights fear being controlled or harmed by others.

What motivates a type Eight? Their biggest motivation is the need to be in control, powerful, and invulnerable to external forces. They want to have enough power, energy, and resources to protect themselves and others (especially the underdogs). Eights are also driven by the need to impact and stand for something meaningful.

Wings:

Type Eight has the Seven-Wing, which is "The Maverick," and the Nine-Wing which is "The Bear."

Arrows and their meaning:

Type Eight has two connecting arrows, namely 2 and 5. When moving in the direction of disintegration and stress (five), self-confident Eights suddenly become evasive and fearful like unhealthy Fives. However, the arrow pointing to growth and integration (two) shows a lustful, controlling Eight transforming into a more caring and warm-hearted individual like a healthy Two.

Examples of famous people:

Some well-known people sharing the enneagram Seven include Winston Churchill, Martin Luther King, Jr., Saddam Hussein, Aretha Franklin, Pablo Picasso, Frank Sinatra, Mae West, Barbara Walters, Clint Eastwood, Jack Nicholson, Serena Williams, Donald Trump, Alec Baldwin, Franklin D. Roosevelt, and Ernest Hemingway.

Type Eight levels of development:

There are different expressions of type Eights that you'll need to learn. At various stages of development, a type Eight will exhibit certain behavior and attitudes depending on how disconnected they are from their higher Self. Let's look at each level.

Healthy levels

Level 1 is a type Eight at their highest and best. Here the individual possesses excellent levels of self-control and feels very connected to their higher self. This Eight has cultivated and developed their gentle caring side, and they have a deep sense of gratitude and joy. They are magnanimous, merciful, courageous, and generous. They are willing to put themselves in serious jeopardy to achieve their vision and have a lasting influence.

Level 2 is where type Eight is strong, powerful, self-confident, and assertive. They have a strong inner drive to accomplish their goals and meet their needs and wants. They know how to stand up for what they envision and have an unbeatable "can do" attitude. And they do all this from a place of emotional stability and self-restraint.

Level 3 is where an Eight is pretty decisive, authoritative, and commandeering, always wanting to be the person others look up to. This individual takes the initiative and knows how to make things happen. Consider them a champion of the people, a provider, and protector. They carry themselves with honor and integrity, and they enjoy championing others as well.

Average levels

Level 4 is where the Eight begins to deny their own emotional needs. Self-mastery, especially of their emotions, isn't yet attained. They are, however, very hard-working, resourceful, and self-sufficient. At this point, the Eight is more concerned with financial independence and having enough resources to live life on their own terms. This individual is typically quite rugged, enterprising, and pragmatic.

Level 5 is where we see the oppressive aspects of an Eight taking over. This individual wants to control their environment and the people around them. There might be quite a bit of boastfulness, pride, and egotism in their demeanor as they attempt to impose their will and vision on others. At this point, the Eight doesn't see that equality anymore, and the internal disconnect and emotional conflict are more significant, so they will have difficulty respecting others.

Level 6 is the level of development where an Eight is aggressive, intimidating, and confrontational. This individual will have plenty of adversaries. They won't be afraid to issue threats and reprisals to get obedience from others. They might even go as far as instilling insecurity and fear in others to tame them, which creates plenty of resentment and hostility. Competition is the name of the game, and they believe everything is a battlefield and emotions are for the weak.

Unhealthy levels

Level 7 is where a type Eight spirals downward into the dark side of their personality. This Eight is hard-hearted, immoral, and in some cases, pretty violent. In an attempt to control everything and everyone, they usually turn into ruthless dictators in their own right.

Level 8 is when the Eight becomes too reckless and over-extends themselves. In an attempt to feed their power-hungry addiction, they take actions that scare and even hurt those around them. They might develop delusional ideas about their power, feeling omnipotent and unstoppable, which often causes them to make grievous mistakes.

Level 9 is rock bottom for a type Eight. This Eight has the emotional range of a teaspoon, making them stone-cold, antagonists who are highly antisocial. At this point, the individual is vengeful, almost barbaric in their thoughts and actions, and will destroy anything and everything that doesn't conform to their will.

Addictions:

To cope with the emotional and psychological turmoil this type faces, especially at those unhealthy levels of development, Eights might resort to alcoholism, tobacco, and other narcotic substances for relief. They also tend to ignore their physical and emotional needs even if they feel an issue.

HOW TO RECOGNIZE IF YOU'RE AN ENNEAGRAM EIGHT

Let's look at some easy-to-spot traits for an Enneagram type Eight, and make sure you take note of how many you identify with. Bear in mind that some of these traits will be more pronounced in healthy Eights while others will be more present in unhealthy Eights.

- You vehemently despise being controlled or manipulated in any way.
- Vulnerability is something you seriously struggle with, even when it's someone with whom you're intimately involved.
- Your attitude can sometimes come off as intimidating and abrasive even when you don't mean to. But that doesn't bother you much because you feel the world absolutely needs people like you.
- Though you don't usually express it openly, nothing gives you as much joy as seeing the people you've taken under your wing thrive and prosper in life.
- You refuse to enable self-sabotage or self-pity in the people you love. That's why you're not afraid of giving a little tough love from time to time, especially to those you care about.
- When backed up against the wall, your first instinct is to tackle it head-on single-handedly.
- You hate asking for help or relying on others.
- Leading others and taking the initiative come naturally to you. And something about your personality just seems to compel others to follow your lead.
- You have a great deal of respect for those who show resilience, courage, and perseverance in the face of adversity.
- If you had a mantra, it would probably be "you create your own luck through hard work, a strong character, and relentless pursuit."
- You believe respect should be earned through competency and reason, not status or age.

STRUGGLES AN ENNEAGRAM EIGHT MIGHT HAVE

Impatience

You have a keen sense that time is limited, and you want to make the most of your time on earth accomplishing as much as you can. That's a great driver, and it enables you to make things happen. But it can also create a lot of impatience, especially with people who seem slow. Procrastinators and time-wasters tend to get on your last nerve, and they might not enjoy the reaction they get from you. While it is great to be so motivated, becoming too impatient with yourself, others or conditions beyond your control can be detrimental. Learn to trust in the process.

Dominating or even intimidating others without meaning to

As stated earlier, the need to be in charge, in control, and to lead the way comes naturally for an Eight. Even at the most healthy levels of development, you'll still need to keep this trait in check so that others don't feel too controlled by you. This aspect is pretty pronounced and tends to suffocate others when it comes to the more average and unhealthy Eights. I know you don't like sugarcoating anything or coddling people, but you'll need to be mindful of how straight and direct you are if you don't want to come off as offensive. The struggle is real because sometimes you'll feel like you're being forced to choose between being your authentic, bold self and playing diplomat (which you can't stand). Still, I encourage you to be mindful of your reactions. Take time to consider the effects of your reactions, especially when dealing with relationships you deeply value.

Putting too much pressure on yourself

With so much strength, power, boldness, ideas, and the belief that you can make the impossible a reality, it's easy to go too hard on yourself. Eights are notorious for physical and emotional self-neglect, especially at average and unhealthy levels. You might feel like you don't need help from anyone or that you can't afford to slow down and take a break because the mission is too critical. Here's the thing, to build a lasting legacy, you'll need all the help and rest you can get. Rest and relaxation are equally as important as going hard. And even though you struggle to delegate, feel vulnerable, or do anything in a less than perfect way, understand that these are not signs of weakness. I encourage you to give your-self permission to stop running all the time and just enjoy healthy downtimes regularly.

Struggling with emotions and the V-word

If there's one word that gets you all conflicted, it's got to be - vulnerability. You might have associated vulnerability and emotions with weakness for a long time. Having heart-to-heart conversations is probably one of the hardest things you can do, even with the people you care about the most. Your strength and independence seem to be at odds with compassion, gentleness, and vulnerability. Many Eights often worry that others might take advantage of them or try to control them if they openly share their feelings. Start slow if you realize it's hard to let someone in (as is often the case with many Eights). Open your mind enough to start developing that level of intimacy and tenderness with just a few people who earn your trust over time. Don't feel forced into it but do put some effort so that it can actually happen. Being vulnerable with another, even if it's just one person, will ulti-mately make you stronger and more grounded. It can be scary, but it's always worthwhile.

GROWTH TIPS FOR EIGHTS

#1: Prioritize self-care

This is one of the most significant shifts I encourage you to make immediately. Make time each day to do something that grounds you and brings you into the awareness of the self. Neglecting your body, mind, emotions, and higher self only weakens your power and creates unnecessary hurdles on your path of greatness. Think about this, you have big plans and require boundless energy to make those dreams a reality. How do you source this energy? Where will it come from in unlimited ways? Average Eights assume they can rely on external stimulants to keep them going. That is not only very detrimental, it's also quite temporary and unreliable. There is a better way, and that is through self-care rituals and time spent connecting with your higher self. You will need to create a routine that incorporates practices that serve all three domains of yourself, i.e., body, mind, and spirit. Find things you enjoy doing like sports, swimming, massages, etc., to take care of your body; feed yourself nourishing mental food to take care of your mind, and take up practices like yoga, Tai Chi, and meditation to nurture all three domains. The more these three are working harmoniously, the more unstoppable you become.

#2: Connect with your thoughts and emotions

As a body or gut-based type, you tend to act out of instincts which is excellent but not holistic. You might notice a big shift in your temperament just making this one move - reconnect with your thoughts and feelings before taking action. When you combine all three, i.e., gut, thoughts, and feelings, your decisions and actions will be more accurate and powerful.

#3: Open yourself up to unconditional love

The tendency is to view people as strong or weak, with you or against you. This way of thinking can make you intensely loving to your close friends and family members but numb you out when it comes to so-called strangers. Unfortunately, that can make it difficult to establish solid relationships built on trust and mutual respect. To do big things, you'll need a lot of people working with you, and the best way to lead these people and gain their loyalty is through love rather than intimidation and force. Practicing unconditional love and recognizing that you can give and receive love more freely will liberate and empower you. It will strengthen your professional and personal connections. I know you like everything to be on a merit-based system but make love the exception to this rule.

#4: Prioritize rest and downtime

Work hard and remember to rest enough too. Schedule downtime and sleep time just as you do work time. All great decisions, ideas, and actions occur when a mind is refreshed, sharp, and alert. Listen to your body and give it ample resting time not based on what others say but solely based on what your mind and body tell you is right for you. Some people like Kevin Hart can operate sharply on four hours of sleep, while others like Gary Vee need seven hours. There's no right or wrong here. Just make sure you do what's suitable for your body.

TYPE 9: THE PEACEMAKER

Overview of type Nine:

Type Nines are commonly referred to as peacekeepers or even mediators because they value peace and harmony above all else. These individuals are unselfish, easy-going, and very amicable. All

Nines prefer to avoid conflict, making them somewhat withdrawn from life in varying degrees. Some Nines are introverted, so it's easier for them to isolate and avoid anything that threatens their peace of mind. Others lead more active and social lives, but even then, you'll always see a degree of disengagement and lack of involvement as if they are trying to insulate themselves from threats.

For the most part, Nines will be optimistic, supportive of others, and adopt a "go with the flow" attitude at all times. They enjoy being outdoors and trying their best to live in serene environments. Although Nines appear conservative, they can still be highly resilient in the face of change and uncertainty. As a matter of fact, most Nines are more resilient and open to change than they think. One unique struggle this type experiences far more than any other in the Enneagram typing system is their tendency to lose themselves in personal relationships. Often they will take on the characteristics of their partner and completely mute out their own unique qualities and voice. That makes it easy for a Nine to mistype themselves. Mothers can also give themselves up to the family entirely and lose their unique identity causing them to mistype as a Two. And while that dissolving of one's self is driven by the need for harmony, it often breeds resentment and anger, which periodically explodes. Even though it's not easy to spot, Nines don't like outer control, just like type Eights. The only difference is, they don't show it upfront. Instead, they show their resistance passively, resulting in passive-aggressive behavior.

At work, type Nines will get along with everyone and genuinely see each person's perspective, making it easy for others to feel understood. They will, however, do everything possible to avoid or end conflicts around them.

Different types of Nines will view the world based on their level of development, but as a general rule of thumb, healthy Nines are: calm, honest, supportive, and use their natural conflict diffusing superpowers to maintain harmony and social fluidity in every setting.

Unhealthy Nines are lethargic and struggle significantly with procrastination. They may become overly passive and highly self-critical.

Within the Centers of Intelligence triad, type Nines fall into the "Gut" center alongside type Eights and Ones. The core unresolved emotion for this triad is anger. Although Eights are excellent at expressing their anger and Ones resist it, Nines prefer to avoid it altogether. Their only focus is to find inner peace.

A healthy type Nine will come across as agreeable, gentle, kind, calm, stable, honest, accepting, optimistic, creative, and trusting. These are actually pretty distinct qualities that one would easily observe in type Nines. This type has the natural superpower of healing conflicts around them without much effort. They are also great persuaders, and others easily listen and follow their advice.

At their best, Nines are sturdy unifying individuals who bring people together and heal disputes.

Core Desire: To have complete inner stability and peace of mind.

Core Fear: Nines fear separation and loss

What motivates a type Nine? The need to find inner and outer peace and harmony. Nines want to avoid conflict at all costs.

Wings:

Type Nine has the Eight-Wing, which is "The Referee," and the One-Wing, which is "The Dreamer."

Arrows and their meaning:

The type has two arrows, namely 3 and 6. When moving in the direction of disintegration and stress (six), Nines becomes anxious, stressed, and worried like unhealthy Sixes. However, the arrow pointing to growth and integration (three) shows a self-neglecting and lethargic Nine transforming into a more energetic, purpose-driven individual like a healthy Three.

Examples of famous people:

Some well-known people sharing the Enneagram type Nine include Walt Disney, Audrey Hepburn, Sophia Loren, Kevin Costner, Queen Elizabeth II, Abraham Lincoln, Carl Jung, Janet Jackson, George Lucas, Lisa Kudrow, Tobey McGuire, John F. Kennedy Jr., George W. Bush and Ronald Reagan.

Type Nine levels of development:

There are different expressions of type Nines that you'll need to learn. At various stages of development, a type Nine will exhibit certain behavior and attitudes depending on how disconnected they are from their higher Self. Let's look at each level.

Healthy levels

Level 1 is type Nine at their best. This individual is self-possessed, fulfilled, and at one with all. They have great autonomy, equanimity and enjoy a deep sense of contentment with who they are and life as a whole. Having found that inner peace and authentic self, they are able to form deeper connections with others and facilitate great healing all around them. People naturally trust in and follow their sage advice. This Nine is alive and deeply connected to themselves and others.

Level 2 is where the Nine is emotionally stable and serene. Their level of trust is high, and they approach life, relationships, and challenges with ease and an unshakable calmness. This type Nine is receptive, accepting of themselves and others, totally unpretentious, patient, and genuinely lovely with people.

Level 3 is an optimistic type Nine who is still aware of their persuasive and healing superpower and uses it positively to harmonize groups and bring people together. This individual is reassuring, supportive, a strong communicator, and excellent at mediations.

Average levels

Level 4 is where a type Nine starts idealizing others and going along with whatever people say whether or not they agree. They tend to deflect things and have trouble speaking their truth, especially when they aren't sure whether it will be well received.

Level 5 is still an active but somewhat disengaged Nine. This individual is unreflective and a little absent-minded. Those that are social and outgoing will still be around people. Still, they won't be responsive to other people's problems choosing instead to walk away. For the most part, this type Nine is "tuned out" and oblivious because they would rather be indifferent than exert themselves or focus on problems that will only heighten their inner issues.

Level 6 is where type Nine prefers to minimize problems and seek peace at any price. That means they will agree with things just to maintain peace and even resign themselves in matters where they feel nothing can be done to create change. We also start to witness a lot of procrastination in the individual as they prefer to put off anything in the real world that adds to their inner disturbance and instead turn to wishful thinking and magical solutions.

Unhealthy levels

Level 7 is where a Nine takes a downturn to the dark side of their personality. The person is stubborn, obstinate, and feels powerless. They isolate and disassociate themselves from all conflicts to the point where they can walk away and leave someone else in danger just to avoid getting caught up in the conflict.

Level 8 is where the type Nice seeks ways of blocking out anything that causes conflict in their world. They are numb, neglectful, and depersonalized in all their interactions wanting nothing to do with an inharmonious world or environment.

Level 9 is where the type Nine can barely focus on any task as lethargy, powerlessness, and self-criticism kick into high gear. They suffer from passive-aggressive behavior in whatever existing relationship they have, and most become severely disoriented and catatonic.

Addictions:

To cope with and suppress some of the emotional and psychological unrest that this type faces, especially at the unhealthy levels of development, Nines may resort to alcohol, marijuana, overeating, depressants, and psychotropics. They might also avoid any physical activity.

HOW TO RECOGNIZE IF YOU'RE AN ENNEAGRAM NINE

Let's look at some easy-to-spot traits for an Enneagram type Nine, and make sure you take note of how many you identify with. Bear in mind that some of these traits will be more pronounced in healthy Nines while others will be more present in unhealthy Nines.

- Your biggest desire is to have a world without violence, disease, or anything negative.
- You can't stand seeing sadness in another person.
- Everyone sees you as that genuine friend who is always laid back and easy to be around.
- You have a hard time picking sides in a fight.
- People naturally trust and open up to you.
- You've always been the mediator and peacekeeper in family gatherings.
- You realize your personality tends to shift when you're around certain people. It's almost like you gell and become more like them.
- You're in the habit of dealing with problems by not dealing with them, hoping that by not acknowledging them, they'll somehow just disappear.
- Going through the Enneagram model and identifying your type feels impossible because you see yourself in all of them and can't decide which is the real you.

STRUGGLES AN ENNEAGRAM EIGHT MIGHT HAVE

Indecisiveness

Almost all Nines struggle with decision making especially when several parties are involved. Their natural inclination to maintain peace and harmony can stand in the way of making even the most uncomplicated choice like "do we go for Chinese or Italian?"

It's tough for a Nine to voice their opinion because they are so gentle and caring about others in their life. At average and unhealthy levels of development, this can lead to a loss of identity as the Nine merges themselves with the other (especially a romantic partner). Besides, most underdeveloped Nines have never taken the time to know what they really want. So they might go through life doing things others suggest because they don't know their own personality.

Putting things off because they stress you and take you away from your zen

Procrastination is a huge problem for the less developed Nines. The need to move at a slow, calm speed can sometimes cause them to procrastinate, especially on things that require high energy. Deadlines sound like death to a Nine, and it's easy for overwhelm and lethargy to get the best of them.

Feeling the pressure to give in

Do you ever feel like people are taking advantage of your goodness? Have you been screwed over by friends over and over again? Do you often wonder whether the people in your life love you for who you really are or if they just love you because they need something from you? These are common thoughts for Nines. As troubling and upsetting as it may feel, the main cause of this experience is that you're not feeling safe enough to be your authentic self. It is you who lets people push you over and take decisions on your behalf because you've never emphasized your voice. In the name of politeness, you've said yes even when it was a self-betrayal, and now people have become accustomed to that. But all is not lost. You can still change things for the better without creating disharmony in your life.

Calm and cool on the outside, burning on the inside

Nines are considered extremely calm, but we know their unresolved emotion is anger. So even though you might not see it externally, Nines can harbor a lot of resentment and even rage. Since a typical Nine doesn't want to cause conflict, they'll often remain silent or even bury their opinion if it contradicts what others say. They are often terrified of losing their temper not just because of the external relationship but because they're trying really hard to find and keep that inner peace. If you're a Nine and you've noticed a wave of brewing anger, it's time to grow further along with your personal development and learn healthy ways of dealing with this emotion. Don't repress the anger or resentment. Use the Enneagram tool to heal and cultivate the confidence to speak your truth even if no one else agrees.

GROWTH TIPS FOR NINES

#1: Become aware of your anger

Notice when judgment, resentment, and anger start brewing. As soon as you become tense or irritable, get curious and ask yourself, "what underlying issues have just been triggered?" If you can label and tame the issue, it will get easier with time. But even if you can't get a clear answer, I encourage you to find healthy ways to voice that emotion instead of suppressing it.

#2: Ask for time to make your decisions

Indecision is a big struggle for you so, train yourself to become a better decision-maker. Start with small things like deciding beforehand where you want to go for dinner with friends this weekend. When they ask and throw around suggestions, give yours as well. If someone at work asks you to choose something at a moment's notice and you need time to think, rather than say "whatever you want," request some time to think it over. This will take practice, but the more you do it, the better it gets.

#3: Share your interests, values, and ideas with others

Make a vow to yourself right now that you'll stop placating others just to avoid conflict or that uncomfortable feeling in your stomach. And once you make that commitment to yourself, start taking an interest in the things you enjoy. Try different things and when you find something you genuinely like, let the people you care about know even if they don't like that activity. When you have a new idea or someone steps on your values, make it known. Have the courage to speak up with kindness and candor (yes, these two qualities can go well together). Given your calm demeanor, you'll have an easy time disagreeing with someone and voicing your truth without necessarily triggering their nerves. Trust that your peacemaking superpower can enable you to transform into a peaceful warrior. And if you're worried about losing friends and loved ones - don't be. The people who love you already know how good you are. Showing up as more of yourself will only increase their respect and love.

#4: Set mini targets daily

As you continue to work on your personal development, set mini-goals of things you'd like to accomplish. Write these down and select definite completion or due dates. Keep a small list of short to mid-term targets and an even smaller list of daily things you want to accomplish. As you complete an important project or hit a target, reward and celebrate yourself. This small change in how you approach your life can have a tremendous shift in your energy and overall growth.

PART TWO
YOU AND THE ENNEAGRAM

CHAPTER 8

DISCOVERING WHO YOU REALLY ARE

After going through the contents of section one, you likely have an idea of which personality type most represents you. If not, that's okay. Sometimes, finding yourself in the Enneagram system requires more thought and brutal self-analysis. As a matter of fact, I always encourage everyone to read all nine types comprehensively before taking the test to identify their own type. Realize that we all have a basic personality type but learning about all nine enables us to understand ourselves and others better. It's also essential to see the connections from one type to another because regardless of our number, there's a tiny facet of other types existing in us.

On this quest for self-discovery and uncovering more of your true Self, we're going to approach this on two levels. First, we help you figure out your core type - pretty straightforward and easy to do.

Second, we dive deeper to uncover - who you really are. Have you ever asked yourself, "who am I?" If so, that second level won't be as scary, and you'll likely pick up a few new insights to add to your current understanding. For those who've never pondered this simple yet profound question, get ready for an awakening that will set you on the right path of self-discovery. Let's not get ahead of ourselves here. First things first, how do you figure out your core type?

IDENTIFYING YOUR ENNEAGRAM

There are countless tests that you can take to determine your enna type. The most common one is the Riso-Hudson Enneagram Type Indicator (RHETI) and is considered by experts to be among the best with about 80% accuracy. You can also take the TAS questionnaire. I will include links in the resource sections for some of the recommended online tests, many of which are paid. If you don't yet want to pay for a test, you can ponder specific reflective questions to gain more clarity about your type.

- How do you react to stress, strangers, happy or unpleasant situations on a daily basis?
- What's a predominant underlying emotion that you just can't shake for as long as you can remember? Is it mostly fear, shame or anger?
- What are some defining qualities or character traits that you and others associate with you?
- What is your worldview and frame of mind? Could you spot some of your thought patterns in any of the enneagram types?

The key to identifying your type is 100% honesty.

You need to identify which driving emotions and basic fears guide most of your behavior. That way, you can avoid basing your type purely on outer traits. So let's briefly go through each of the nine fears as listed by Don Riso and Russ Hudson in their book "The Wisdom of The Enneagram":

- Type 1 fears being evil or corrupt.
- Type 2 fears being unloved or unwanted by others.
- Type 3 fears being unaccomplished and worthless.
- Type 4 fears losing or not finding their identity and expressing how unique and different they are.
- Type 5 fears being inadequate, incompetent, and helpless.
- Type 6 fears being without guidance and support.
- Type 7 fears pain and deprivation.
- Type 8 fears being controlled and harmed by others.
- Type 9 fears loss and separation.

Most of us will have more than one basic fear. Still, as I said earlier, through observation, you'll recognize the dominant basic fear and underlying emotional theme that's ever with you no matter where you go.

Once you've identified the triad with the primary unresolved emotion and the dominant basic fear, you'll easily find the corresponding number, and the rest should fall into place. Your basic fear will feel most intense, pervasive, and maybe even a little horrifying. You might start to recognize it showing up as different experiences in different domains of your life.

The Enneagram Test:

Getting an online test is always recommended. It gives you a comprehensive understanding of your personality, blind spots, thought patterns and validates your existing ideas about your right enneagram type. So, even after identifying your type, I want to encourage you to take an online test. If you go on Google to find an Enneagram test, you'll be flooded with countless options, some of which aren't very good. The best one is the "Riso-Hudson Enneagram Type Indicator" created by The Enneagram Institute. Please check the resources section for the links I recommend.

WHO ARE YOU REALLY?

The whole point of studying personality types and taking an enneagram test is to know who you really are. Most people lack the courage to begin this quest, and understandably so. It's scary and hard. Our society doesn't encourage us to figure out our true selves at a young age. Instead, we are encouraged to complete and be like others around us. The social norms around what constitutes a respectable, successful human being are pretty vain and shallow. Own a fancy car, get a high-paying job, mortgage a home, buy the latest shiny gadgets, and have an Instagram-perfect life - then we consider you a successful human being. Unfortunately, this is anything but a successful life.

Martin was successful by this shallow measure of society. By the age of twenty-nine, he'd mortgaged his first house, married a beautiful wife, and drove his dream car. Martin also had a corner office at his firm and frequently vacationed at the Hamptons. It took an illness, losing his job, and getting a divorce for Martin to realize that he really didn't know himself at all. When he finally hit rock bottom, he was fortunate enough to come across Deepak Chopra's books and online content, which forced him for the first time to ask the questions "who am I? What do I believe in? What is my purpose in life?" These questions served as a launchpad for his journey of self-discovery. It took a lot of work on his part and much therapy, meditation, study, and daily reflection, but Martin was finally able to transform his life and reconnect with his true Self.

What is the difference between the true Self and the ego-self?

Your ego self or everyday self is the you that gets mixed up with daily stuff. Within you lies a deeper, wiser, and more powerful self who is often a silent observer. If you pay attention, you'll realize that Self. How will you know it's your true Self? In the same way, you can identify the difference between salt and sugar. Each possesses certain qualities, and as you taste them even with a blindfold, you can pick them apart. The same is true for your ego-self and your true Self. When you experience the qualities of your true Self and learn to cultivate them as part of your well-being, you'll quickly tell when you're operating from the everyday self or the higher Self.

- *The true Self is stable and secure.* Ever had those moments where you just felt more solid than a rock and sound in your thinking? You had tapped into a quality of your higher Self. Your higher Self is ever reliable and secure, but your ego-self is constantly shifting.
- *The true Self is always at peace.* There's an inner knowing that all is well that's only possessed by your true Self. On the other hand, your ego is easily disturbed, doubtful, agitated, and tumultuous.
- *The true Self is clear and sure about things.* In every moment, no matter what you face, your higher Self knows what step to take next. Unfortunately, the opposite may be said for your ego, who is ever confused, easily distracted, and influenced by outer circumstances. Again, there's a fundamental knowing that's only possessed by your higher Self.
- *The true Self is love.* We can quickly identify this quality because most of the time, living from the ego's perspective, we seek love outside of us. We become

dependent on outside sources and people to make us feel loved. That's a clear sign we're not living from the true Self. When you live from your true Self, there's no void to fill, no loneliness or loss, and you don't seek to find love. Instead, you long to give from your overflow.

Looking at these qualities, you can start figuring out what perspective you live from on a day-to-day basis. And that becomes a good indicator of how much development you need to unlock your highest and best Self. In the Enneagram types, we discussed the different levels of development so that you could know what to work on to rise to the highest level where you get to live primarily from your higher Self. That doesn't mean you destroy or deny the ego-self. It means you've transformed it into its healthiest version, where it serves your Soul and life's purpose.

Our society operates mainly at average and lower levels of development where that connection to the true Self is significantly severed. That's why negativity seems to win the day, and our actions are more selfish, ruthless, and divisive. But once we can each learn to recognize and encourage the qualities of the true Self to rise within us, positive change will take place. All it takes is one individual taking on that responsibility in their life to expand their awareness, make better choices, and know more about who they really are. By reading this book, you have made that choice for your life. As long as you keep asking the right questions and move forward in your path of self-discovery, you'll not only positively impact your life but also those around you.

10 QUESTIONS TO HELP YOU DISCOVER MORE ABOUT YOUR PERSONALITY

Although the quest of finding your true Self cannot be completed by a simple questionnaire, answering the following questions will offer a clear starting point, bring in some new perspective and guide you on the next steps. These questions were developed by Dr. Phil and curated by Lifehack (Chui). Fire up your word document or notes, and let's begin. You'll find the points for each question and what they indicate at the end of the questions.

Question 1: When do you feel at your best?
a) in the morning
b) during the afternoon or early evening
c) late at night

Question 2: You usually prefer to walk...
a) fairly fast, with long steps
b) fairly fast, with little steps
c) less fast head up, looking the world in the face
d) less fast, head down
e) very slowly

Question 3: When talking to people, you...
a) stand with your arms folded
b) have your hands clasped
c) have one or both your hands on your hips or in pockets
d) touch or push the person to whom you are talking
e) play with your ear, touch your chin or smooth your hair

Question 4: When relaxing, you sit with...
a) your knees bent with your legs neatly side by side
b) your legs crossed

c) your legs stretched out or straight

d) one leg curled under you

Question 5: When something really amuses you, You react with...

a) a big appreciative laugh

b) a laugh but not a loud one

c) a quiet chuckle

d) a sheepish smile

Question 6: When you go to a party or social gathering, you...

a) make a loud entrance, so everyone notices you

b) make a quiet entrance, looking around for someone you know

c) make the quietest entrance, trying to stay unnoticed

Question 7: When you're working or concentrating very hard, and you get interrupted you...

a) welcome the break

b) feel extremely irritated

c) vary between these two extremes

Question 8: Which of the following colors do you like most?

a) red or orange

b) black

c) yellow or light blue

d) green

e) dark blue or purple

f) white

g) brown or gray

Question 9: When you're in bed at night, in those last few moments before drifting, you lie...

a) stretched on your back

b) stretched out face down on your stomach

c) on your side, slightly curled

d) with your head on one arm

e) with your head under the covers

Question 10: You often dream that you are...

a) falling

b) fighting or struggling

c) searching for something or somebody

d) flying or floating

e) you usually have dreamless sleep

f) your dreams are always pleasant

Points for each question

1. (a) 2 (b) 4 (c) 6
2. (a) 6 (b) 4 (c) 7 (d) 2 (e) 1
3. (a) 4 (b) 2 (c) 5 (d) 7 (e) 6
4. (a) 4 (b) 6 (c) 2 (d) 1
5. (a) 6 (b) 4 (c) 3 (d) 5 (e) 2
6. (a) 6 (b) 4 (c) 2
7. (a) 6 (b) 2 (c) 4
8. (a) 6 (b) 7 (c) 5 (d) 4 (e) 3 (f) 2 (g) 1
9. (a) 7 (b) 6 (c) 4 (d) 2 (e) 1
10. (a) 4 (b) 2 (c) 3 (d) 5 (e) 6 (f) 1

Now add up all the points to see your result:

OVER 60 POINTS

Others see you as someone they should "handle with care." You're seen as vain, self-centered, and one who is extremely domineering. Others may admire you, wishing they could be more like you, but don't always trust you, hesitating to become too deeply involved with you.

51 TO 60 POINTS

Others see you as an exciting, highly volatile, rather impulsive personality, a natural leader, one who's quick to make decisions, though not always the right ones. They see you as bold and adventuresome, someone who will try anything once, someone who takes chances and enjoys an adventure. They enjoy being in your company because of the excitement you radiate.

41 TO 50 POINTS

Others see you as fresh, lively, charming, amusing, practical, and always interesting; someone who's constantly in the center of attention but sufficiently well-balanced not to let it go to their head. They also see you as kind, considerate, and understanding, someone who'll always cheer them up and help them out.

31 TO 40 POINTS

Others see you as sensible, cautious, careful, and practical. They see you as clever, gifted, or talented, but modest. Not a person who makes friends too quickly or easily, but someone who's extremely loyal to friends you do make and who expects the same loyalty in return. Those who really get to know you realize it takes a lot to shake your trust in your friends, but equally that it takes you a long time to get over it if that trust is ever broken.

21 TO 30 POINTS

Your friends see you as painstaking and fussy. They see you as very cautious, extremely careful, a slow and steady plodder. It would really surprise them if you ever did something impulsively or on the spur of the moment, expecting you to examine every-thing carefully from every angle and then usually decide against it. They think this reaction is caused partly by your careful nature.

UNDER 21 POINTS

People think you are shy, nervous, and indecisive, someone who needs looking after, who always wants someone else to make the decisions, and who doesn't want to get involved with anyone or anything! They see you as a worrier who always sees problems that don't exist. Some people think you're boring. Only those who know you well know that you aren't.

How many points did you get?

A TIP FOR FINDING YOUR TRUE SELF

While personality tests and questionnaires are a great starting point, always remember that your true Self is far greater and that it takes a lot more than just identifying your personality. Use them as clues but never stop there. The deeper you go, the more you'll uncover the real you. One great approach that's been helpful in my quest has been the emphasis on finding what's meaningful to me. I learned this from reading Viktor E. Frankl's book "Man's search for meaning," which transformed how I approached my life. Frankl survived some of the most horrific circumstances during the Nazi war. He was held prisoner in the Nazi concentration camp and witnessed his entire family killed, including his wife and kids. The fact that he survived was mainly because he could maintain a sense of meaning. Frankl said, "Life is never made unbearable by circumstances, but only by lack of meaning and purpose."

How does that help us in our quest for self-discovery?

The more we seek our personal sense of purpose and live from a grounded place of personal values and the principles we hold true for ourselves (uncorrupted by society and parental influence), the closer we are to living from our true Self. But don't assume that will be an easy feat.

It's one thing to understand your personality and identify the traits and quirks that make you - you. But without a deeper cleanse of the influences that have shaped that personality and the ability to see who you are underneath that social cloth, you'll struggle to access that grander "Self" that we discussed earlier. Purpose and meaning seem to be the summoning energies that draw out that higher Self. Perhaps that's why people like Viktor Frankl, Nelson Mandela, and others were able to endure things our egos consider impossible. They were living from their true Self, not their personalities, which made all the difference in the world.

CHAPTER 9
SUBTYPES PART 1

Something strange will occur as you get familiar with the enneagram personality typing system and start using it to understand yourself and others. One of these days, you'll come across someone of the same ennea type, yet they'll act totally different. The first time that happened to me, I thought the system was broken, or the person had mistyped themselves. Turns out, neither of those was accurate. We shared the same Enneagram type but differed significantly in our expressions, mainly due to our subtypes. In subsequent chapters, we'll cover what subtypes are, why they matter, and the different subtypes for each Enneagram type.

WHAT ARE ENNEAGRAM SUBTYPES?

Subtypes are rich, nuanced ways of understanding more about yourself and the things that influence your behavior. They combine your Enneagram type and natural instincts, i.e., how you're wired for survival. They are commonly referred to as instinctual subtypes or instinctual variants and have everything to do with your basic survival instincts. Why would we care about survival instincts in today's modern society? We may not be hunters and gatherers or at the risk of being eaten by a lion on our way home from work, but that part of our brain is still active and operational. The drivers and motives that enabled us to navigate those dangerous times still influence our day-to-day experiences more than we know. Perhaps that's why we can see a highly educated, well-dressed politician behaving like a caveman. Instead of pretending that your instincts aren't there, it's better to become more aware of how they influence your reactions. The more awareness you have about your subtypes, the easier it will be to bring them into balance and create alignment with your higher Self.

THE THREE INSTINCTUAL SUBTYPES:

The three classifications are self-preservation (SP), social (SO), and sexual (aka intimate or One-to-One). We all possess each of the three instincts, but a dominant one combines with our specific Enneagram type to form a subtype. Let's look at the difference between these three subtypes. Think of it in the same way that you have two arms, but one is more preferred and is likely why you refer to yourself as either right-handed or left-handed (depending on which arm you rely on most). In the case of subtypes, you have three, but one is more influential, and you use it as your default setting. Most of us can quickly identify the dominant instinct. We might, however, feel indifferent or neutral about the second place instinct and barely recognize the third and least influential instinct.

Self-preservation (SP)

As the name suggests, self-preservation is about prioritizing physical needs such as food, shelter, health, family, and finances. In other words, safety and security is the top priority here. Most of the focus goes into preserving resources and energy as the strategy for basically getting through life and feeling safe and protected. If you have this instinct as your dominant one, you tend to prioritize family, physical, and mental well-being. You likely manage your energy levels and resources in ways that help you avoid becoming overwhelmed or too stressed.

Social (SO)

Social instinct prioritizes belonging and being accepted by the group or community. It's about working toward shared goals with others as the strategy for getting through life and feeling safe and protected. If you have this as your dominant instinct, you most enjoy being part of a group or working in a team with others who share a common goal. You value feeling that you belong and that you're wanted by those in your group. Your focus is often on how others respond to you, and you're quick to notice your standing in any particular group setting. Feeling connected to others and to the greater good matters to you.

Sexual (SX)

As the name suggests, sexual or intimate instincts prioritize connecting one-to-one with individuals. It's about creating a spark or "chemistry" with others. Please bear in mind that the connection doesn't have to be of a sexual nature; it can and often is purely platonic. If you have this as your dominant instinct, you value passion, excitement, and intimacy. You likely have boundless energy, love activities, and experiences that enable you to bond with another individual. Perhaps you tend to seek out friendships and relationships that complete you somehow and offer you that sense of security and safety as you go through life.

Which instinct stood out most for you? Think about how your subtypes are stacked into first, second, and third positions.

Instinctual stacking and counter types:

The subtypes are yet another way of deep diving into who you really are (derived from the model of Claudio Naranjo's system). We all have an instinct stacking whereby one is overused, another is underused, and another still is totally neutral. Shifts may occur at different phases in our lives to switch between the neutral and overused instinct (e.g., when you face challenging circumstances). But in general, we tend to stack them in a particular order which gives rise to the specific way we express our Enneagram type. Knowing which instincts drive your reactions can be an invaluable way of transforming your character and managing your energy. Why is this helpful? Because when your emotional patterns or "passions" and your dominant instinctual drive come together, they create a particular focus of attention that usually reflects a unique insatiable need that drives your behavior.

We study subtypes because they reflect the three different subsets of the patterns of the nine types creating even more nuance in our quest to describe and understand ourselves and others.

You also need to know that for each Enneagram type, there's a countertype. A countertype is a cool way of naming the subset that goes against the main energetic direction of the "passion" for any given enneagram type. This is especially important if you're having difficulty identifying your enneagram type. People who don't seem to fit into any stereotypical enneagram type often have the countertype subtype. That means their dominant instinct clashes with their Enneagram type's emotional pattern (passion), resulting in atypical behavior. Notice, however, that the individual's motivation would remain the same (e.g., if fear is a big thing for that type and their stereotypical behavior is to be phobic, the countertype might clash, causing the person to deal with that fear by taking bold risks). That might cause the individual to mistype themselves. Still, if they go back to the basic desire, fear, and unresolved emotion in their intelligence center, they will find their real enneagram type even if they express it differently.

HOW TO FIND YOUR ENNEAGRAM SUBTYPE:

Now that you understand the basic concept behind subtypes, you're ready to engage in the practical work of identifying your subtype. The best way to do this is to first read through the 27 subtypes and notice what resonates. It's also a good idea to become more mindful as you go about your daily duties in the coming days. Where does your attention go, and what things matter to you? As you go to work or any social gathering, pay attention to what you're noticing and prioritizing. Do you place a lot of value in one-to-one connections or the entire group? When you walk into a room, are you often quick to notice the setup of the place, exit signs, temperature, fire extinguishers, etc.? These clues show you which instinct is dominant in your life. There's no wrong or correct answer here. The goal is self-awareness and self-discovery. If you're still feeling lost and confused, try asking people you trust for their objective opinion about you once you're done going through the subtypes.

∾

THE ENNEAGRAM TYPE ONE SUBTYPES

Self-Preservation One: Worry

The Enneagram One's primary desire is to be good and live with integrity. Dissecting the subtle nuances of SP One, this subtype is often plagued with worry. Their basic fear is to be corrupt or evil. They have a pattern of anger.

Self-preserved Ones are the true perfectionists. They suppress their anger through hard work and rigid rules, all in an attempt to produce perfection. This subtype represses anger the most and has the uncanny ability to transform the heat of anger into warmth resulting in a friendly, benevolent character, especially when operating at those healthy levels of development.

Some characteristics of the Self-preservation One:

- Tendency to be a control freak over their own life.
- Often suppresses anger or resentment.
- Kind and gentle when at healthy to average levels of development.
- Focuses on predicting the future.
- Strives for perfection all the time.
- Tendency to be too hard on themselves.
- Strives to be forgiving, compassionate, and tolerant of others.

Social One: Non-adaptability

In an attempt to be good and manage the fear of becoming corrupt or evil, this subtype enjoys reforming and advocating for change. Social Ones believe themselves to be perfect.

They focus their energy on being the perfect role model they can be through doing things "the right way." Typically possessing a teacher mentality, there's an unconscious need for superiority. In expression, their personality type is more of a cool intellect with a strong need for control. These type Ones are pretty rigid, idealistic and tend to seek out leadership roles within a group so they can show "the rest" how to do things right. Social Ones can be extremists and highly judgemental at unhealthy levels with unrealistic standards for themselves and others. They are also pretty stubborn, argumentative, and stubborn.

However, a Social One is ethical, conscientious, discerning, and helpful at healthy levels.

Some key characteristics of the Social One:

- Tendency toward idealism.
- Strong opinions and convictions.
- Lives by example and enjoys being a role model for others.
- Skilled at reasoning.
- Tendency to take things personally.

Sexual One: Zeal

By now, you know all Ones desire to live in integrity and fear being evil or corrupt. But how is this impacted when we layer on the richness of the sexual subtype? As the countertype for the Enneagram One, Sexual Ones are idealistic and passionate, but their drive is purely focused on improving others (especially their partner/s) and the world at large. They tend to be more reformers than perfectionists and seek to find those who share their ideals and convictions.

Unlike the other two subtypes, this type One isn't afraid to show anger. In fact, they usually act out their anger through their intense desire to improve others. They possess a strong sense of entitlement and believe they have a right to change society and get what they want because they have a higher understanding of the truth. As the countertype for type One, this individual will express their character as more impulsive, pushy, irritated, outwardly angry, and typically goes against the "counter-instinctive" tendency of repressing anger and impulses stereotypically associated with type Ones. Unhealthy sexual Ones are controlling, jealous, pushy, and entitled. They can even go as far as punishing themselves in unhealthy ways to purge themselves of desires they view as immoral (remember, moral perfection is of great importance to this enneatype). Healthy Sexual Ones are more compassionate and pragmatic. They still have high morals but know how to temper their idealistic visions and ideals.

Some characteristics of the Sexual One:

- Idealistic and passionate.
- Determined and brave.
- Tendency to be impatient.
- Often orderly and responsible.
- Prone to jealousy.
- More focused on perfecting others rather than themselves.

CHAPTER 10

SUBTYPES PART 11

THE ENNEAGRAM TYPE TWO SUBTYPES

Self-preservation Two: Privilege

Enneagram Two's primary desire is to be loved for who they are. Their basic fear is being unwanted or unloved. They have a pattern of pride. In dissecting the subtle nuances of type Two, this subtype is perhaps one of the more challenging to identify because pride isn't apparent. It's the countertype of type Two, meaning they behave in atypical ways. As such, self-preserved Twos "seduce" like a child would in the presence of grown-ups. It's their way of inducing others to take care of them. A self-preserved Two adopts a youthful stance as a way of getting special treatment beyond childhood. This Two desire to be loved, prioritized and treated with privilege for being who they are, not because of what they give to others. In expression, their character will be playful, charming, irresponsible with very little pride.

Some characteristics of the Self-preservation Two:

- Playful, warm and childlike.
- Want to be taken care of but fear depending on others.
- Tendency to mistype or appear like type Sevens.
- Idealize people, especially at the beginning of relationships.
- Want to be loved just because they exist.
- Commonly drawn to pleasure and fun.
- More guarded than the other two subtypes in Enneagram Two.
- Fear of rejection caused this subtype to become withdrawn and hurt.
- Extremely tender and emotionally expressive.

Social Two: Ambition

In their endeavor to be loved and manage the fear of being unwanted, this subtype enjoys identifying and connecting with the influential people around them.

Social Twos are seducers who take pride in being perceived as influential leaders and attaining their audience's attention. Pride is an undeniable trait in this subtype Two. As the name suggests, this individual desires to be "on top," beloved, and receive advantages and benefits corresponding to their lofty position. They tend to be quite competitive and less sensitive to other people's emotions compared to the other subtypes within this Enneatype.

Similar to the Enneagram type Three, Social Twos want to stand out and be successful. They can go to great lengths to reach their goals and make an impact. But in keeping with the core desire of all Enneagram Twos, goals still revolve around being loved, wanted, and included in the group (unlike a typical Three whose goal is to be the ultimate achiever).

So, although Social Twos are giving and affectionate, that benevolence comes with expectations. In expression, you'll observe a lot of pride and less than altruistic generosity. Unhealthy Social Twos are manipulative, exploitative and enjoy gossip a little too much. Healthy Twos, however, are charming, empathetic, loving, and generous.

Some characteristics of the Social Two:

- Hardworking and competitive.
- Strives to stand out.
- Tendency to be more introverted than the sexual or self-preservation Two subtypes.
- Aims to be close to those in power.
- Less empathetic than the other subtypes in the group and highly aware of their public image.

Sexual Two: Seduction/Aggression

By now, you know that all Enneagram Twos desire to love and be loved for who they are and they're very afraid of being abandoned or unwanted. But how is this impacted when we layer on the sexual subtype?

Well, Sexual Twos tend to invest all their energy in key individuals intending to forge intimate, passionate connections. They enjoy giving lots of attention to people and aren't shy of employing classical seductive methods to attract those who will meet all their needs.

Sexual Twos are aggressive in their seduction. Unlike the self-preserved Two, they possess a more adult-like approach because they want their needs met and want to have some power.

Besides their need to gain affection and closeness, these individuals are also great listeners taking great pleasure in having intimate conversations about the struggles of a friend or partner. They genuinely believe love conquers all, but underneath that passionate exterior is deep-seated anxiety about their desirability. They depend on their charm to win others over, receive validation and love as a way of solidifying their self-worth.

In expression, this Two's character is energetic, irresistible, and inspires great passions and positive feelings, all for the sole purpose of getting their needs met in life. Unhealthy Sexual Twos are pushy, demanding, and really prone to possessiveness, jealousy, and obsessive behavior. Healthy Sexual Twos, however, are deeply romantic without any ulterior motives. They ooze unconditional love.

Some characteristics of a Sexual Two:

- Charming and highly seductive.
- Less ashamed of having needs than the Self-preservation or Social Two subtypes.
- Generous and supportive.
- Aims to form strong intimate bonds.
- Caring, nurturing, empathetic, and loving unconditionally.

THE ENNEAGRAM TYPE THREE SUBTYPES

Self-preservation Three: Security

Enneagram Three's primary desire is to be desirable and highly successful. What they fear most is failure or a feeling of worthlessness without achievement. As the countertype of Enneagram type Three, these individuals will work hard, strive for success and covertly seek admiration and recognition. Even though they sense their vanity, they try very hard to conceal and deny it.

SP Threes are more concerned about being good people, not just "looking good." That, however, doesn't mean they're not interested in being the "best" in whatever they do. If anything, their concept of being the best is tied to hard work and modesty. They possess a strong code of honor and a need to be self-reliant and hard working. A self-preserved Three will care about their image and cultivate virtues that model the qualities they believe shape a good human. They can also combine material success with hard work and even service to others.

Some characteristics of the Self-preservation Three:

- Wants to be the best at everything.
- Believes in earning admiration from others through hard work.
- Typically mistypes themselves as a Six or One.
- Avoids talking about their achievements or successes in life.
- Works hard to attain a certain level of security.

Social Three: Prestige

In their endeavor to be successful, desirable, and accomplished while managing the fear of failure or a sense of worthlessness, this subtype works hard to maintain a powerful public image. Social Threes only care about one thing - moving up in the world. They are the most competitive and aggressive of the Enneagram type Three. Social Threes are driven by the need to be the best, whether in school, a group setting, or at work. Vanity is present and evident in these Threes, and they very much enjoy the spotlight. With plenty of charm, great energy, focus, and desire to accomplish their goals, social Threes tend to do well for themselves and typically possess a sales or corporate mentality. At unhealthy levels, Social Threes are desperate for attention and validation from others. They will go to any lengths to receive recognition and live to impress others by any means necessary. That often leads to unhealthy and reckless choices. Conversely, a Social Three is pretty inspiring at healthy levels and more of a visionary that people love to follow. Their energy, competency, and charm quickly rally people behind their grand visions.

Some characteristics of the Social Four:

- Charming.
- Highly competitive.
- Skilled at networking and forming strategic relationships.
- Cares deeply about their public image and social status.
- Success and goal-oriented.
- High levels of confidence.

Sexual Three: Charisma

By now, you know all Threes desire to be successful and fear failure or being perceived as worthless. But how is this impacted when we layer on the richness of the sexual subtype? Unlike Social Threes, who are mainly focused on career success and being seen by their community as influential, Sexual Threes are more interested in personal attractiveness. They have a strong desire to be desirable, alluring, and wanted by others, especially their ideal mate.

Sexual Threes neither flaunt nor deny their vanity. Instead, all their energy goes into creating an attractive, irresistible outer image. Often seen as supporters of others, Sexual Threes like to use their charm to promote and please others, especially those they want to win over to their side. As a result, their innate skills and power are often less obvious to others, as are their true intentions. It's a more subtle form of influence because, in the end, they still get to accomplish their goals by putting others first and making them feel more important. Many people mistype this Sexual Three as a type Two because of how supportive, helpful, and people-pleasing they are. Still, closer observation will reveal this individual is more focused on being attractive to others, not necessarily meeting the emotional needs of others.

Unlike the SP Three or Social Three, this type Three isn't focused on money or prestige. Instead, that energy and desire for accomplishment will be redirected to personal appeal and magnetism. However, underneath all that attractive exterior is a deep sense of emptiness. Sexual Threes have a hard time practicing self-love or acknowledging their own strengths. Sexual Threes are vain, narcissistic, jealous, and vindictive at unhealthy levels. They typically get addicted to the pursuit of sexual encounters to feel attractive. Conversely, healthy Sexual Threes are self-accepting, self-improving in mind and body, inspiring, and supportive. They can focus on their own desires and live authentically instead of hiding behind the guise of "supporting others."

Some characteristics of the Sexual Three:

- Enthusiastic.
- Longs to be desired and attractive to others.
- Tendency to people please to get what they want.
- May use their talents and strengths to support and uplift others.
- Long to be and find the perfect lover/partner.
- Often insecure about themselves but won't show it.

THE ENNEAGRAM TYPE FOUR SUBTYPES

Self-preservation Four: Tenacity

The Enneagram Type Four's primary desire is to be authentic in every way possible and to find their true identity. They fear most that they are flawed and lack a true identity. With self-preservation being the countertype of the Fours, they express their pattern of envy through atypical behavior. Rather than dwell in envy and feeling defeated, SP Fours focuses on going after their objects of desire.

Healthy and average SP Fours will be persistent, goal-oriented, creative, resilient, empathetic, and highly self-aware. They have a lot of endurance and are willing to take the initiative to actively seek out the authentic life and material security that's missing. Instead of accepting that void, these individuals will attempt to fix themselves.

From an emotional standpoint, this Four is likely more stoic in the face of pain and doesn't share their feelings as much. Instead of dwelling in jealousy, SP Fours will work hard to get what they lack, making them a bit more masochistic than melodramatic.

Some characteristics of the self-preservation Enneagram Type Four:

- Unlike the rest of the Fours, SP Four works hard to gain the things they desire.
- They dislike complaining.
- Empathetic and compassionate with themselves and others, especially those in healthy and average levels of development.
- Want to be loved because they demonstrate strength and steadfastness.

- Can be Self-absorbed and self-rejecting if they operate at unhealthy development levels.

Social Four: Shame

The social Four is the classic individualist who enjoys being involved and sociable. They enjoy forming close bonds but struggle with envy and jealousy, easily succumbing to these negative emotions. Driven by the basic desire to discover their true identity, live authentically, and the fear of lacking significance in this world, this subtype struggles with shame and rejection a lot.

Unlike the SP Four or the Sexual Four, this subtype is much more sensitive and dwells a lot on their perceived "ingrained flaws." They are melancholic and often lament about their inferiority and how different they are from others. In a group setting, the person constantly compares themselves to others and shows how much they are "lacking" in something. That said, they possess a certain charm that others find appealing which is why they get by in social settings. The deep sense of sadness for this subtype causes them to use pain and suffering as a way to attract attention and affection, hoping that it will bring in their savior to rescue them from their condemned existence. At unhealthy levels, pain and suffering are greatly amplified, and these social Fours tend to play the victim role all the time. However, at healthy levels, social Fours are creative, loving, curious, profound, and empathetic.

Some characteristics of the Social Four

- Tendency to compare themselves to others.
- Struggles to care for their own needs.
- Socially friendly and charming in their own way.
- Tendency to play the victim, especially at unhealthy levels.

- Experiences guilt over wanting things or wanting to fit in.
- Feels like a misfit wherever they are.
- Highly sensitive and keenly focused on their emotions.
- Wants recognition.

Sexual Four: Competition

By now, you know all Fours desire a sense of authentic identity and fear having no significance or identity in the world. But how is this impacted when we layer on the richness of the sexual subtype? Unlike the SP Four or the Social Four, who are often overwhelmed by sadness, the Sexual Four mostly battles anger. Because of this, they tend to mistype as Eights because of how intense and emotionally "hot" they come across.

Sexual Fours deny their suffering and try to suppress their shame. Their focus is mainly on making others feel worse than they do in an attempt to feel better. That's why these Fours come across as competitive and dramatic. They actually want to be the best and most elite in their chosen passion-based endeavor. This Four takes the power of others as a personal challenge, and their value is ever fluctuating depending on who they are comparing themselves to. And just like other Sexual subtypes, the Sexual Four longs to be the object of desire to another. But they tend to have mixed emotions, including admiration, envy, and hatred. At unhealthy levels, this will be more pronounced and will, in fact, go to great lengths to be the only person that matters to the individual they're with. Unhealthy Sexual Fours can be pretty wild and have no problem sabotaging other people to get revenge or merely out of jealousy. They can be arrogant, elitist, superior, and hold grudges without good reason. Healthy Sexual Fours are more composed, Self-aware, forgiving, inspiring, and capable of finding harmony between their inner and outer world. They learn to embrace both their individuality and their emotions, even the darker ones, and find better ways of handling them rather than externalizing them in angry outbursts or taking offense.

Some characteristics of the Sexual Four:

- Envious and jealous of other people's success.
- Highly competitive.
- Deeply struggle with feelings of inferiority and crave feeling superior to others.
- Romantic and individualistic
- Highly creative and imaginative.
- More assertive than SP Fours and Social Fours.
- Tendency to externalize their suffering through anger.

THE ENNEAGRAM TYPE FIVE SUBTYPES

Self-preservation Five: Castle

The Enneagram Type Five's primary desire is to be competent and knowledgeable. They fear incompetency and lack of proper resources to maintain their independence. When this ennea type combines with the self-preservation instinct, it causes them to build thick boundaries and isolate themselves to protect their energy and resources. Hence the term "castle" because the behavior expressed is that of creating a little sanctuary of their own making.

SP Fives are the least expressive of the type Fives and do every-thing possible to live within the confines of their resources so they can remain completely self-reliant. This need to have enough supplies behind their castle walls can sometimes lead to hoarding and cause these individuals to be very stingy and aloof. Healthy Fives respect the space and needs of others and don't take from others without giving back in equal measure. Unhealthy SP Fives are stingy and unwilling to open up to others.

Some characteristics of the self-preservation Enneagram Five:

- Typically introverted.
- Tendency to view the world as hostile, intrusive, and overwhelming.
- Intensely private.
- Struggle with their emotions and understanding them.
- Tendency to place a lot of boundaries between themselves and the outside world.

Social Five: Totem

In their endeavor to be knowledgeable, competent, and manage their fear of becoming dependent on others or lacking resources, this subtype seeks to become a master in their field and be the go-to person on a particular topic. The Social Five finds their sense of belonging by being highly skilled and supporting those who need academic help. Most of their social interactions are with people who are drawn to their topics of interest which is usually scientific, philosophical, or educational in some other way.

Although the social Five relates to others in a group, it is always through common interests based on knowledge and shared values rather than emotional connection. They are passionate and hungry for knowledge and understanding the meaning of life. While these Fives are more social than the rest of the Enneagram type Five, they still hate small talk, gossip, or anything that wastes their precious mental or physical resources. Social Fives are condescending, antisocial, and out of touch with reality at unhealthy levels. Conversely, healthy Social Fives are observant, trustworthy, unbiased, logical, authentic, and highly informed.

Some characteristics of the Social Five:

- Want to become someone important.
- Prefer to interact with and engage with people they admire intellectually.
- Socialize with people who share the same ideals.
- Very idealistic.
- Driven to discover the ultimate meaning of life.

Sexual Five: Confidence

By now, you know all Fives desire knowledge and independence and fear being incompetent. But how is this impacted when we layer on the richness of the sexual subtype? Sexual Fives are passionate, intensely imaginative, and might even possess a romantic streak as the countertype for the Enneagram Five. They love creating mental utopias and visions of the ideal partnerships. Sexual Fives long for a mystical union (a merging with someone that results in unconditional love). When they find that connection, they are like an open book. To the outside world, however, the Sexual Five will still remain a mystery, but to their chosen partner, they are transparent, caring, and share all their secrets.

Sexual Fives are the most emotionally sensitive of the Fives. Although they might appear reserved and analytical like the others, deep down, the Sexual Fives are emotionally intense and romantic. Are they a little strange? Sure. But for those who can accept their eccentric ways, these individuals are fantastic. If, however, the Sexual Five feels misunderstood or unappreciated, they quickly recoil and disappear. At unhealthy levels, they are isolated, impossible to please, and prone to dangerous sexual experimentations. Conversely, healthy Sexual Fives are loving, authentic, visionary, wise, and are constantly learning and growing.

Some characteristics of Sexual Fives:

- Deeply imaginative.
- Romantic and sensitive side that isn't quite present in the other subtype Fives.
- Innovative and perceptive.
- Tendency to indulge in lush fantasies.
- Values one-to-one connections.
- Wants to find the ideal relationship.

CHAPTER II
SUBTYPES PART III

THE ENNEAGRAM TYPE SIX SUBTYPES

Self-preservation Six: Warmth

The Enneagram Type Six's primary desire is to have security and guidance. They fear being unprepared to face a situation or lacking proper support. The self-preserved Six is the most "phobic" of all the other Sixes. They express their fear by seeking protection through friendly and protective alliances. This Six strives to be warm, friendly, and trustworthy but underneath that demeanor is deep anxiety. Their focus is on relationships as a means of securing the sense of safety and security that they need in the world, but they constantly worry about losing that alliance, being rejected, and being alone. A self-preserved Six will often get stuck in analysis-paralysis because they doubt themselves and others too much, especially at unhealthy levels of development. Healthy SP Sixes, however, tend to trust themselves more and feel connected to the world around them. The radiate serenity and security that comes from within.

Some characteristics of the self-preserved Six:

- Skeptical and doubtful (increases exponentially at unhealthy levels of development).
- Warm and friendly, especially at healthy and average levels of development.
- Tends to mistype themselves as Enneagram Type Two.
- Oriented toward relationships and personal connections as a survival mechanism.
- Fears letting people down.
- Feels a lot of responsibility and guilt when things go wrong.

Social Six: Duty

In an attempt to feel safe and secure while managing their fear of being unsupported and unprepared, this subtype cares a lot about finding a community or group that they can fit into and feel safe and protected.

Social Sixes are loyal, dutiful, and care a lot about their commitments within the group. They enjoy following rules and guidelines that offer a form of protective authority. Social Sixes want to feel that they are part of something bigger than themselves and are willing to make sacrifices for that experience. They have a tendency to think more about how others will react to their choices and decisions in life, which often promotes analysis-paralysis in their decision-making.

Social Sixes are most comfortable when surrounded by like-minded individuals in a community where everyone helps each other out and wants what's best for the whole. They express their fear as anxiety and cannot stand uncertainty, so they seek to deal with these emotions through abstract reasoning and ideologies. A social Six focuses on precision and efficiency in all their endeavors. Social Sixes are controlling, impatient, judgemental, and self-critical at unhealthy levels. They struggle with passive-aggressive behavior and often question their own beliefs. However, a healthy Social Six is courageous, more confident in their own thoughts, ideas, and beliefs. They are loyal, dedicated, and filled with integrity.

Some characteristics of the Social Six:

- Tendency to seek out rules and structures to guide them.
- Punctual and precise.
- Prefer to rely on authority for protection and guidance.
- Seek to understand and fulfill their role within a group structure.
- Tendency to become a fanatic for their belief system, especially at the lower unhealthy levels of development.

Sexual Six: Beauty/Strength

By now, you know all Sixes desire security, protection, guidance, and fear lacking support or guidance from authority. But how is this impacted when we layer on the richness of the sexual subtype? As the country for the Enneagram Six, this subtype deals with underlying fears by becoming aggressive risk-takers. Sexual Sixes adopt the mindset "me against the world." They do everything possible to fight their fears and hardly ever let their guard down. Sexual Sixes believe that the best defense is a good offense, and they attempt to live by that frame of mind. Because of their constant suspicion and fear of being duped, they can seem like they're always about to explode.

This Six believes in preparation and skill development as a way of staving off both anxiety and their enemies, so they work hard to look good and feel powerful. They do this by building up their strength, both emotional and physical. They often subject themselves to extreme sports that build their endurance. At unhealthy levels, they are erratic, combative, dominating, depressive, and may violently lash out at others. They are often obsessed with watching their perceived enemies for any attack signs. Healthy Sexual Sixes are more chilled, courageous, protective, reliable, and self-reliant.

Some characteristics of the Sexual Six:

- Tendency to be impulsive.
- Often contrarian.
- Extremely loyal and reliable, especially at healthy levels of development.
- Strives to be physically strong and attractive.
- Tendency to run towards fear to fight it off.
- Often mistypes as an Enneagram type Eight.

THE ENNEAGRAM TYPE SEVEN SUBTYPES

Self preserved Seven: Keepers of the castle

The Enneagram Type Seven's primary desire is freedom and happiness. They fear pain, negativity, suffering, or missing out on life. They're also terrified of feeling trapped in situations, relationships, etc., that might cause them to lose their sense of freedom and adventure. The added nuance as a self-preserved Seven is that they'll seek safety and security in material things and networking opportunities.

SP Sevens are great at establishing alliances that are advantageous to their well-being. Pleasure is something they absolutely love and seem to be great at getting their way when dealing with people, perhaps due to their cheerful, charismatic nature. A healthy self-preserved Seven is pragmatic and content with what they have, but the unhealthy SP Sevens tend to be demanding, greedy, and even manipulative.

Some characteristics of the self-preservation Enneagram Seven

- Practical and realistic.
- Highly opportunistic.
- Charming and talkative.
- Skilled at networking.
- Great sense of humor.
- Enjoy having the best and newest material things.

Social Seven: Sacrifice

In an attempt to pursue their desire for freedom and happiness while suppressing their fear of pain or being caged, this subtype is the most idealistic of the Sevens. They are also the countertype in the group, which means they exhibit the opposite behavior of what a Seven would typically express. Hence, while all the other Sevens succumb to gluttony, a social Seven is often altruistic and focused on helping others.

They are keenly aware of their tendency to exploit others and strive to purify themselves of this paradigm by sacrificing their own needs to support others. Their passion is to be perceived as good as they make personal sacrifices. A social Seven will express enthusiasm and idealism as a way of making themselves feel valued and active in the world, demonstrating that they can get by with very little. Often visionary, they see many new opportunities and enjoy finding friends and advisors who share their interests and enthusiasm. Most Social Sevens will position themselves in roles that enable them to work with others to pursue a cause that excites them. That doesn't eliminate their urge to pursue various things and gain further knowledge. At times, their speed can be a bit too unrealistic for others in the group. This can cause a strain as the Social Seven turns impatient and might even consider "moving on" to do things on their own.

At unhealthy levels, impatience and restlessness are high. They become irresponsible, never quite finishing any project they start and scattering their energy all over the place as they jump from one thing to the next. However, at healthy levels, Social Sevens are bold, visionary, adventurous, resilient, and dedicated to their chosen goal. They've learned to tame that inner child and know how to find freedom in commitments.

Some characteristics of the Social Seven:

- Idealistic.
- Enthusiastic.
- Helpful and generous.
- Visionary.
- Fears being excessive or indulgent.
- Craves admiration.
- Capable of taking on great responsibilities.

Sexual Seven: Suggestibility

By now, you know all Sevens desire freedom and happiness and fear missing out or feeling trapped. But how is this impacted when we layer on the richness of the sexual subtype? Sexual Sevens aren't shy of expressing gluttony and do so by imagining better than their current reality. They are romantic dreamers with a passion for living in their imagined states. Some refer to them as overly naive and suggestible because they tend to look at the world through rose-colored glasses. Ever optimistic and lighthearted, everything is possible to a sexual Seven. Their primary focus is experiencing as many pleasurable fantasies as possible. They quickly feel trapped and overwhelmed by the mundane routines of life, so they attempt to create more thrill around them. That often makes them restless and impulsive, embellishing everyday life just so it can seem more intoxicating. Sexual Sevens are fickle, fearful of commitment, and prone to falling for crazy schemes at unhealthy levels. Healthy Sexual Sevens, on the other hand, are joyful, enthusiastic, imaginative, hopeful, and productive. They've learned to be content with everyday life.

Some characteristics of the Sexual Seven:

- Spends more time fantasizing than in reality.
- Trusting and hopeful.
- Tendency to jump from one activity to another.
- Constant search for the next new, exciting and extraordinary thing to bring more pleasure and magic in their life.
- Idealistic and highly imaginative.

THE ENNEAGRAM TYPE EIGHT SUBTYPES

Self-preserved Eight: Satisfaction

The Enneagram Type Eight's desire is to be in control and have autonomy. What they fear is being controlled by others. When it comes to the nuances of a self-preserved Eight, they are practical and willing to do whatever it takes to ensure their needs are met. That makes them pretty aggressive in some cases. They're also not big on small talk or "chit-chat." these Eights like to cut past formalities and niceties and get straight to the point.

Self-preserved Eights express their lust by focusing on their needs and the needs of those they care for. They need to satisfy their material needs instantly and don't handle frustration or disappointment very well. SP Eights are the least expressive of the group and often look for symbols of power and impact such as fancy cars, nice houses, etc. Unhealthy SP Eights can quickly turn into selfish, impatient bullies who stop at nothing to get what they want. On the other hand, healthy SP Eights are strong, protective of others, and enjoy motivating others to reach their dreams.

Some characteristics of the self-preservation Enneagram Eight:

- Practical and realistic.
- Direct in their communication.
- Hardworking and highly productive.
- Exudes a quiet strength.
- Always goes for what they want.

Social Eight: Solidarity

In an attempt to pursue their desire for autonomy and have complete control while managing their deep-seated fear of being vulnerable and losing control, this subtype is the most intellectual among the Enneagram Type Eight. As the countertype of the Eights, these individuals come across as warm and more mellow than the other two subtypes. They deeply value harmonious relationships and friendships. Once loyalty is established, they go above and beyond for their friends, caring for and protecting them against any and all threats. They like to tend to their own needs leading a life of intense action, various activities, and minimal downtime for self-care. Unlike your typical Eight, a Social Eight is often less aggressive and genuinely more helpful. At unhealthy levels, Social Eights are anti-social. They turn self-destructive, reckless, and blind to the damage they cause others. Conversely, healthy Social Eights are charismatic, goal-driven, fearless, self-reliant, and passionate about caring for and protecting those they care about.

Some characteristics of a Social Eight:

- Friendly and charismatic.
- Enjoy debating with others.
- Pursues adventure and thrill.
- Keep busy with different types of projects.
- Stands up for others.

Sexual Eight: Possession

By now, you know all Eights desire control and autonomy, and they fear being vulnerable or controlled by others. But how is this impacted when we layer on the richness of the sexual subtype? Sexual Eights are the most rebellious of the Eights and naturally hate rules. These Eights are intense, charming and they love having control and influence. Rather than seeking material security like an SP Eight, a sexual Eight prefers to get "power" over things and people. Their focus is on becoming powerful and dominating their whole environment. While they can be loving and devoted, they tend to struggle with intimacy, seeing it as a risk that could give control and power to others. Sexual Eights like a challenge and aren't shy of being direct even if it leads to conflict and confrontation. Sexual Eights are possessive, jealous, dominating, and controlling at unhealthy levels. Healthy Sexual Eights are the opposite. They are self-reliant, forgiving, and protective of others, almost to the point of being heroic.

Some characteristics of Sexual Eights:

- More emotional than the SP Eight and Social Eight.
- Pragmatic and enterprising.
- Rebellious and anti-authoritarian.
- Often perceives intimacy as a struggle for control.
- Demands loyalty from loved ones.
- Strives to attain pleasure.
- Action-oriented more than reflective.

THE ENNEAGRAM TYPE NINE SUBTYPES

Self-preserved Nine: Appetite

The Enneagram Type Nine's primary desire is inner peace and stability. What they fear most is conflict and fragmentation, especially internally. All type Nines express the passion for laziness. Self-preserved Nines are more concerned with seeking security and comfort in the material world. They are practical and routine-oriented, preferring to focus on everyday things in the present moment rather than idealism or distractions. Books, television shows, good food, rest and relaxation are very attractive to this Nine, so they invest their energy in these activities. Some are pretty talented, but their focus on immediate minor rewards typically hinders them from pursuing something grand. At unhealthy levels, SP Nines are apathetic and emotionally shut down. They get hooked on their creator comforts and turn a blind eye to everything else in their environment. However, at healthy levels, they are peaceful unselfish, level-headed, and patient.

Some characteristics of the Self-preservation Nine:

- Enjoys predictable routines.
- Prefers and seeks out physical comforts.

- Fun-loving and accepting of themselves and others.
- At times, food and drink are used as anxiety suppressants.
- Prefers to focus on the real concrete world.

Social Nine: Participation

In the pursuit of inner peace and stability, while managing the fear of conflict, disconnection from Self, and fragmentation, this subtype is known for being influential, caring, and giving themselves to others without reservation. Nothing means more to a Social Nine than just being part of a meaningful group. As the countertype of the Nines, the Social Nines are cheerful with a warm exterior. They enjoy participating and prioritizing other people's needs ahead of their own. That's because underneath all that giving is a fear of abandonment and exclusion.

Social Nines most enjoy fusing with groups and work hard to be the fun-loving, friendly, peace-keeping character in the various groups they join. There exists an underlying sense of insecurity regarding their self-worth, which often causes them to "people-please" in an attempt to fit in. At unhealthy levels, Social Nines are needy, insecure, emotionally out of touch with themselves, and tend to fall into depression. Conversely, healthy Social Nines are energetic, thoughtful, non-judgmental, and extremely kind.

Some characteristics of the Social Nine:

- Generously and unconditionally gives.
- Longs to fit in.
- Tendency to overwork or overextend themselves in the group.
- Cheerful and friendly.
- Prioritizes the group needs ahead of their own.

Sexual Nine: Fusion

You know all Nines desire inner peace and fear internal instability or conflict by now. But how is this impacted when we layer on the richness of the sexual subtype? Sexual Nines express their pattern of laziness by merging with the important people in their lives. Unknowingly, this Nine will take on the attitudes, opinions, and feelings of others. While they are kind, gentle characters who typically lack assertiveness, this inability to stand on their own identity tends to backfire in the long run. They often live out their dreams and fantasies through others and spend most of their time imagining their future with other people but nothing else beyond that. Their anger is easily sparked if their relationship with that significant other is threatened, which surprisingly turns them into the sassy, passive-aggressive type. While the relationship they merge with is often intimate, such as with a spouse, it can also be with a best friend or God. Sexual Nines are so tied to another individual that they become self-neglecting, repressed, codependent, and prone to resentment at unhealthy levels. Healthy Sexual Nines, however, are empathetic, comforting, peaceful, and loving from a place of their own true connection and personal identity. They've done the hard work of eradicating the tendency to merge with another's identity and live from their true personality.

Some characteristics of the Sexual Nine:

- Tendency to lack a sense of Self, especially at those unhealthy levels of development.
- Empathetic and emotionally aware.
- Tendency to merge inside relationships and lose their sense of Self.
- Kind, peaceful, and genuinely loves.
- Always prioritizes the needs of others.

- Calm, poised, and possess a powerful presence that can offer a sense of comfort and healing to those nearby.

The Enneagram system is indeed a wealth of information that can at times feel overwhelming. It can feel a little overwhelming when you first encounter these concepts, from standard Enneagram types to triads, wings, and now subtypes. Understand, however, that all these different aspects are nuances that are meant to add richness to your understanding of yourself. By going through the subtypes in this section, I hope you've developed more awareness and understanding of why you navigate life as you do and why someone else in your same Enneatype will appear so radically different. The more you understand yourself, the easier it will be to understand others. Speaking of which, it's time to start applying your knowledge of the Enneagram in practical ways, starting with existing relationships.

PART THREE
DEEPENING RELATIONSHIPS

CHAPTER 12

CULTIVATING HEALTHY RELATIONSHIPS

Relationships are an integral part of our mental, emotional and physical well-being. Research now shows that having healthy, strong relationships can contribute to a long, healthy, and happy life. In contrast, there is compelling evidence that being isolated or alone in life is comparable to the risks associated with obesity, blood pressure, and cigarette smoking. A significant percentage of people who first look to the Enneagram for help are usually driven by the need to improve their personal or professional relationships. So in this chapter, we'll focus on how you can improve your personal relationships. In the next chapter, we'll focus on work relations.

WHY HEALTHY RELATIONSHIPS MATTER

A review of 148 studies found that people with strong social relationships are 50% less likely to die prematurely (Kreitzer, RN, Ph.D.). And that's not all. Being in a healthy committed relationship is linked to less production of cortisol (a stress hormone) and faster healing. Studies show that recovering from an illness or procedure happens faster for long-term partners than for single patients. Of course, it's not just about surviving hard times. It's also about cultivating great habits together, and again, having a healthy relationship is linked with a healthy lifestyle. Think about it; if you're in a relationship with a lover or best friend who takes up all your free time and they are into eating healthy, exercising, and developing their mind, you're more likely to pick up those habits as well. It's much easier to take on new healthy habits when the people around you do the same. So there's no denying that relationships influence our lifestyles, and the quality of that relationship affects our well-being. Author Brené Brown explains, "A deep sense of love and belonging is an irreducible need of all men, women, and children. We are biologically, cognitively, physically, and spiritually wired to love, to be loved, and to belong."

Can the Enneagram really help?

Kaley Warner openly shares how the Enneagram helped save her marriage. Let's hear it from her own words.

"I was a newlywed. I had moved to New Jersey and was struggling. My husband was in a Ph.D. program, and I felt isolated. I had left all my friends and found the prospect of making new ones daunting. My husband and I had a bike crash, and the physical and mental toll from those tangled handlebars hung heavy over us. His energy was gone. I was escaping my pain through working harder and traveling. The more critical and demanding I become of him, the more he checked out. We were reaching an impasse. I remember telling a friend that he wasn't the man I fell in love with and married. I'm sure I wasn't the woman he wanted to share his life with either. That winter, while home for the holidays, my mom suggested that we attend the same Enneagram training she and my dad had attended a few years earlier. I don't remember the details of how she did it, but Nate and I both thought it was our idea to go, and so we registered.

In a small room in Atlanta, as Russ Hudson described each of the Enneagram Types and the intricacy of the system, I felt like I was being reminded of something I already knew. Everyone, he said, just made sense. The Enneagram described patterns of people's behavior that I'd seen in my life better than anything else I'd learned. When he got to Type 1, my husband laughed with recognition. And I cried. Russ put words to the invisible experience of my life. He explained my inner critic and striving for perfection in a way that didn't make me feel judged but understood. All of my attempts to improve our marriage that had instead been driving us apart came to light. I had been trying so hard but creating the opposite result. As I learned about my personality, there was grace for myself that I hadn't experienced before. When Russ got to Nate's type, the same thing happened, only in reverse. I laughed; understanding the behaviors that had just the day before made me angry. And Nate cried, having his inner experience articulated in such a way that we now shared a vocabulary to discuss what had been happening. We spent the rest of the training in deep conversation about our types, how we had been triggering each other and how we could appreciate the other person instead of getting lost in the conflict. "

— KALEY WARNER KLEMP

HOW THE ENNEAGRAM WILL HELP YOU DEEPEN AND HEAL YOUR RELATIONSHIPS

As with the story above, the Enneagram works because it's a perfect tool for communication with another. As you understand yourself and the other person, you can use a common language to address existing conflict, pinpoint the triggers and unhealthy habits, and genuinely learn to see the world through the lens of the other. So if you've struggled with relationships in the past or if you don't even know what kind of relationship would be right for you, it's time to understand how your strengths and weaknesses affect your personal relationships. Take responsibility for the energy you bring to any relationship, and things will change for the better. Used properly, the insights you're learning throughout this book will naturally aid you in cultivating healthy relationships.

ENNEAGRAM TYPE 1 - THE PERFECTIONIST IN RELATIONSHIPS

Type Ones are sticklers for rules and doing things the right way. Achieving perfection is a huge driving factor, and these individuals know what they want every time. In relationships, Ones are loyal, dedicated and want the relationship to move in a specific direction.

If you're a type One, perhaps you'll notice friction arises when dealing with types who are more ambiguous and less interested in structure. You're incredibly organized, tend to see the world in shades of black and white, and you're uncompromising in your strong moral code.

Your strengths include being faithful, conscientious, and focused on personal growth.

Your weaknesses in relationships include being too critical, controlling, and uncompromising. You might be placing too high expectations on your partner. In an attempt to make everything perfect, you could drive a wedge between you.

How to improve:

To bring out the best in you and others, embrace a little bit of spontaneity, playfulness, and creativity. Tell your partner or friend what you need instead of expecting them to read your mind. Find ways of relaxing and hit the snooze button on your rules from time to time, especially on things that you know will bring joy to your partner, friend, child, etc. For example, let your kid have ice cream before dinner if he's been such a good boy all summer, and allow your partner to surprise you with an unplanned weekend getaway. It's okay if you get lost and miss a reservation at your favorite restaurant.

What you need:

As a One, you need a partner that can encourage you to become a bit more playful and relaxed. Someone who can add a bit of spontaneity into your life in ways you enjoy. Someone who understands and respects your need for perfection and rules but still facilitates fun in your relationship.

ENNEAGRAM TYPE 2 - THE GIVER IN RELATIONSHIPS

Type Twos are nurturers, helpers, and love supporting others. In relationships, they'll put others first, even if it comes at the expense of their own needs.

If you're a type Two, perhaps you've realized that it's easier for you to give love and attention to another, but it's not so easy to provide the same to yourself. I want to remind you that one can never pour from an empty cup. The more you fill yourself up first, the more you'll naturally have to give to those you care about.

Your strengths include knowing how to make people feel loved and appreciated.

Your weaknesses in relationships include becoming possessive and too dependent on your partner. It might also be that you struggle with self-care.

How to improve:

To bring out the best in you and others, resist the urge to fix everyone's problems. Sometimes you just have to sit back and allow others to solve their issues. And make sure you prioritize self-care and, when needed, put yourself first, even if that means saying no to another's request. Those who love you will appreciate and respect your decision to first tend to your own needs.

What you need:

As a Two, you need a partner who will respect, appreciate and show you how much they love you just as you are. Your romantic partner should encourage you to create healthy boundaries and tend to your own emotional well-being.

ENNEAGRAM TYPE 3 - THE ACHIEVER IN RELATIONSHIPS

As a type Three, I can tell you we put a lot of time and energy into career, achievement, success, and building legacy. In relationships, Threes want to be appreciated for their hard work and accomplishments. Sometimes this can be too extreme to the point of emotional neglect, which leads to unhealthy behavior patterns.

I want to remind you that you can have thriving relationships and a successful career. If you're a Three, perhaps you're now becoming aware of how obsessive you can get with your work and accomplishments. You just need to realize that your value isn't tied to your achievements. The people in your life who love you will love you for who you are if you can just carve out a little time to be present with them.

Your strengths include high energy, charisma, creativity, and an eagerness to live up to others' expectations.

Your weakness in relationships includes being impatient, too self-absorbed, absent-minded, and too focused on your career at the expense of your personal relationships.

How to improve:

Find a way to be there for the people who love you that you want to nurture in your life. It is possible to strive for success, meet your emotional needs, and spend time with your loved ones. Customize a plan that works for your particular situation and, as much as possible, have some downtime where you can switch off from work stress and just have fun with those who love you.

What you need:

As a Three, you need a person who can encourage and support you in taking care of your emotional needs. A romantic partner that can help you unwind and gives you compelling reasons to put work on mute for a little while and just connect with each other.

ENNEAGRAM TYPE 4 - THE INDIVIDUALIST IN RELATIONSHIPS

Type Fours are the sensitive, creative types who care more about living authentically than fitting into society. In relationships, they want to be understood and appreciated for their uniqueness and individuality.

If you're a type Four, it's time to let go of this tension that causes you to feel alone, misunderstood, and inherently flawed. That doesn't mean that everyone will "get you." It means some will, and it's essential to remain open and positive enough to recognize when you come across the few that will accept, embrace, appreciate and love you in all your uniqueness.

Your strengths include being empathetic, intuitive, romantic, playful, and open to new experiences. You have a natural gift of understanding how your partner really feels, and you probably want to find a partner who can reciprocate that.

Your weaknesses in relationships include a tendency to be quite moody and dramatic. Some Fours are also needed, super sensitive to criticism, and are prone to recurring cycles of depression.

How to improve:

Learn to balance that common emotion of sadness and melancholy with gratitude and hopefulness so you can bring positive energy into the group.

What you need:

As a Four, you need a romantic partner who is open, understanding, Self-aware, and expressive in their appreciation of you and all that you are. The more emotionally stable and in-tune your partner is, the richer your connection will be.

ENNEAGRAM TYPE 5 - THE INVESTIGATOR IN RELATIONSHIPS

Type Fives are thinkers. They prefer to observe in the safety of their own privacy, preferably where very few can access. Generally introverted, most Fives prefer isolation and appear secretive and mysterious, but once they find their partner, they become an open book, often sharing everything with their chosen one. If you dig deep, some Fives might even have a romantic streak in relationships. They do, however, require enough time alone to process, think and reset even from their loved ones.

If you're a Five, perhaps you've noticed how hard it is to relate to others. You might be thinking that being isolated and detached is the best solution. I want to remind you that a truly fulfilling life comes from enjoying all that life offers. That includes healthy relationships as well. The meaning and understanding of life that you seek cannot be found if you neglect your emotions or deny yourself the possibility of having a few thriving relationships.

Your strengths include being a curious lifelong learner, kind and perceptive. Your keen interest in activities that foster growth and satisfy your thirst for knowledge can be highly appealing to someone with shared interests.

Your weaknesses in relationships include being aloof and withdrawn from the world. You might also have a tendency to become cynical and irritated with a partner, especially when they interfere with your space or drag you out of your comfort zone.

How to improve:

To bring out the best in yourself and others, open up some more to your chosen partner and allow yourself to sometimes tread outside your comfort zone (thoughtfully, of course).

What you need:

As a Five, you need a partner who is comfortable giving you as much time as possible to yourself. Someone with similar passions in life who isn't afraid to talk about "deep stuff."

ENNEAGRAM TYPE 6 - THE LOYALIST IN RELATIONSHIPS

Type Sixes are known for their loyalty, integrity, dedication, and honesty. They like to know that they're in a steady, secure relationship.

If you're a Six, it's time to start trusting yourself first and foremost. It's easy to go through life being skeptical and mistrusting of everyone, and there's value in having that alert mind. But don't let it ruin your entire existence. Slow down and breathe before responding to others. That will help you get out of your head and make grounded decisions. Make this your truth: The world isn't all bad. In fact, many good, honest people desire to connect with me."

Your strengths include being trustworthy, dependable, supportive, warm, committed, and interested in long-term relationships, even if they're purely platonic.

Your weaknesses in a relationship include defensiveness, being too self-conscious, and struggling to trust others quickly. Some Sixes can turn anxious, fearful, insecure, and controlling.

How to improve:

Work on building your self-confidence and self-esteem. The more you feel good about who you are and come to learn your true worth, the less insecure you'll feel around your partner. Enneagram experts also suggest increasing your capacity to be vulnerable. Brené Brown's book "Daring Greatly" might be a great starting point if you want to strengthen yourself while embracing vulnerability simultaneously.

What you need:

As a Six, you need a trustworthy partner who will be loyal to you. Someone who recognizes how valuable you are and isn't afraid to be vulnerable with you and play the long game in your romantic relationship.

ENNEAGRAM TYPE 7 - THE ENTUSIAST IN RELATIONSHIPS

Enneagram type Sevens are energetic, passionate, full of ideas, and almost always happy. These are the people who have this electrifying energy that you just want to be around. In relationships, they bring that special spark and know how to have a good time.

If you're a Seven, being optimistic and open-minded comes naturally. Perhaps you've noticed, though, that in your quest for novelty and freedom, you're struggling to build anything substantial. Being future-oriented is excellent, and I know you love only the best in life. I want to encourage you to find strength, freedom, and power in the present moment as well. Learn to be more mindful and patient with yourself. When hardships come, (and they will) allow you the grace to explore rather than escape those feelings. If you genuinely want to live life fully, you must learn to experience it all (the please and the pain).

Your strengths include spontaneity, enthusiasm, great positive vibes, and adventure.

Your weaknesses in relationships include a tendency to be narcissistic, distracted, and unable to stay committed in any relationship. Perhaps you have difficulty finishing any project you start, and your partner often complains you have a short attention span.

How to improve:

Work in finding that balance between adventure and stability. There is a way for you to have both. Freedom and commitment do go hand in hand if you just change perspective. Suppose you can resist the urge to run away or abandon ship, whether things get tough. In that case, you'll finally start experiencing the joys of a committed relationship.

What you need:

As a Seven, your best romantic partner is someone stable, confident, patient, and someone willing to guide you as you slow down in life. Trust your partner enough to let them be serious and weigh in once in a while, especially on important matters.

ENNEAGRAM TYPE 8 - THE CHALLENGER IN RELATIONSHIPS

Enneagram Eights are confident, naturally rebellious, and contrarian, but they are pretty outgoing. In relationships, they can be very protective of their own to the point of arrogance.

If you're an Eight, perhaps you've noticed how hard it is for you to put down your guard and become vulnerable with another. Even intimacy scares you a little, doesn't it? Your ability to see dynamic power plays in every relationship is a gift, but don't let it become a curse. I want to encourage you to let someone in. Remember, not everyone is out to take advantage of you or control you in any way.

Your strengths include being honest and direct in your communication which is great for any kind of relationship. You also tend to be generous, supportive, and extra protective of the people you care about.

Your weaknesses in relationships include being too demanding, uncompromising, too intense, and wanting to control everyone and everything. That can really choke your romantic partner and create a disconnect between you.

How to improve:

Being vulnerable doesn't make you weak. It strengthens your relationship. Work on allowing your softer side to show, at least to your romantic partner. You should also improve your active listening skills and allow your partner to weigh in on matters that concern you both.

What you need:

As an Eight, you need a romantic partner who loves your intense energy and shares your passions and vision in life. Someone who loves how fierce you are and cheers you on.

ENNEAGRAM TYPE 9 - THE PEACEMAKER IN RELATIONSHIPS

The Enneagram Nines are peaceful, kind, gentle, and excellent mediators. In relationships, they often play the supportive, gentle, non-judgmental role.

If you're a Nine, you've got an extraordinary gift, and it's time to use it. Your ability to see all sides in any conversation make your presence powerful and an antidote for many conflicts. However, that doesn't mean that all conflicts are destructive. Instead of turning a blind eye or avoiding them at all costs, cultivate more of your confidence and increase your self-mastery so that you can serve others without losing yourself. Find your voice, live your truth and become the inspiration you were born to be.

Your strengths include being easy-going, calm, loyal, stable, and emotionally sensitive to your partner's feelings.

Your weaknesses in relationships include being passive-aggressive, stubborn, defensive, and at times resentful. Perhaps you've noticed that you've lost your identity in this relationship. That's a common occurrence for a Nine that turns them into people pleasers just to avoid conflict.

How to improve:

Not all conflicts have to end in an argument. There's always a way to maintain peace, even during a disagreement. Work on having healthy conflicts and learn to see the value in expressing your ideas even if they aren't pleasant.

What you need:

As a Nine, you need a romantic partner who will support you and encourage you to speak up and find your voice.

WHICH ENNEAGRAM TYPES PAIR WELL TOGETHER?

Although I don't believe in a "perfect match" because relationship success is based on two individuals and the work they put in, Enneagram experts do have suggestions. The idea behind this Enneagram compatibility isn't to restrict one type to only engage with someone from a specific type but rather to make them aware of the common trends and patterns they've observed. Given how granular the Enneagram system can get and the fact that it focuses more on underlying motives rather than outer behavior, I believe any two types can get together and produce a happy, healthy, thriving relationship. In the book "The Enneagram in Love & Work, researcher Helen Palmer notes that her study uncovered combinations that are more common than others. However, it's important to mention that the research did not consider the combination's satisfaction or compatibility. And what are these common combinations?

Type Ones naturally pair well with Twos and Sevens.

As the detail, oriented, conscientious perfectionists, Ones are drawn to those who can help them lighten up and find beauty in the imperfect moments of life.

In a One-Two romantic partnership, the nurturing, attentive Two can bring a certain warmth to a rigid and task-oriented One. Type Two can help encourage a type One to be more soft and relaxed even as they courageously pursue their perfect ideals in the world. Likewise, type One can bring a sense of structure, security, and consistency to the Two. That can be super appealing for the Two as they often struggle with abandonment issues. These Enneagram types also happen to share wings, so they'll notice some overlap in their traits.

In a One-Seven romantic partnership, the two types connect through their Enneagram Line. Ones might be attracted to the adventurous, joyful spirit of the Seven. This is especially great in helping the hardworking, self-restrained One to let loose and just have fun. Likewise, Sevens might find One's sense of purpose and direction quite attractive. It helps the Seven feel grounded.

Type Twos naturally also pair well with Threes and Eights.

One of the key areas we identified for improvement in type Two is prioritizing and even vocalizing their own needs. Having a romantic partner who can reciprocate intimacy, encourage self-care and not take advantage of the Two's generosity is vital.

There's a high energy match in a Two-Three romantic partnership because these two share similar charisma and interests. The charming Threes often galvanize the Twos to reach their potential instead of focusing on others. Likewise, Twos support the Three with unconditional love and approval, which helps them feel more confident in just being themselves rather than struggling to prove themselves to others through work or status.

In a Two-Eight romantic partnership, these two share an Enneagram line and create a natural attraction. The Twos like the strength, passion, intensity, and conviction that the Eight brings to the relationship. It encourages them to step up and embrace their own power. Likewise, the Eights find this kind of connection appealing because being around a Two enables the Eight to let down their walls and embrace that gentle, loving, and softer side they tend to hide. Twos are excellent at facilitating this vulnerable kind of affection which is super essential for a healthy Eight to have.

Type Threes naturally also pair well with Nines.

Type Threes have a strong image-oriented personality, hindering their vulnerability and authenticity. In a Three-Nine romantic partnership, a calm, poised and stable Nine can enable the Three to accept themselves for who they are, not what they can do. This shift from outer success to inner self-worth reconnects the Three to their emotions. Likewise, Threes help the easy-going Nine move toward the spotlight and find respect and value in their self-identity.

Type Fours naturally pair well with Fives and Nines.

Fours are artistically inclined, highly self-aware, emotionally sensitive, and reflective. They love authentic people who are living their unique truth.

In a Four-Five romantic partnership, the emotionally expressive Fours find comfort in the naturally occurring "straight-talking" no b.s nature of type Five. The "logic first" frame of mind that a Five possesses is very appealing and grounding for a type Four.

Why? They admire how authentic and unafraid Fives are in exploring deep things in life, whether science, emotions or art.

In a Four-Nine romantic partnership, the Fours ignite passion back into the mellow Nines, creating an intensity that can be pretty thrilling for the Nine. Likewise, the Nine is appealing to a Four because of their gentle, non-judgmental nature. This kind of self-acceptance is very appealing to a Four who struggles with emotions and finding their identity.

Type Fives naturally pair well with Ones and Twos.

Besides the compatibility with a type Four, these objective, intellectual Fives also commonly pair well with Ones and Twos.

In a Five-One romantic partnership, the Fives are very attracted to the Ones' curiosity, independence, and integrity. When they find a mutual interest, there can be an instant connection. Likewise, the One's appreciate the Five's lack of judgment and commitment to lifelong learning and improvement. Their partnership can build a strong foundation of trust and dependability.

We're witnessing a true "opposites attract" scenario in a Five-Two romantic partnership. The emotionally attuned and loving Two wouldn't be considered viable for an objective, intellectual Five. Yet it happens more often than you might think. The Two's are very attracted to the Five's firm boundaries, independent and objective nature. Also, knowing how much alone time Fives need, the Twos are better able to self-care and tend to their own needs. Fives also benefit from this connection because having a Two around creates a cozy, domesticated atmosphere that colors the Five.

Type Sixes naturally pair well with Nines.

The loyal, trustworthy, security, and stability-oriented Sixes benefit most from a stable and drama-free relationship. In a Six-Nine relationship, they can have all that and more. The gentle, accomodating, and peaceful presence of a Nine is very soothing for a Six. Likewise, this kind of partnership creates that predictable routine-like connection that Nines find most appealing.

Type Sevens naturally pair well with Nines.

It seems many of the Enneatypes fine Nines naturally irresistible, including the enthusiastic, playful, and adventure-seeking Sevens. In a Seven-Nine romantic partnership, an upbeat and positive atmosphere is created when the agreeable, always peaceful Nine hooks up with the free-spirited Seven. Nines are great at helping Sevens slow down and enjoy the present moment more, which is critical for a healthy Seven. Likewise, the energetic Seven ignites a fire in the often passive and too chilled Nine.

Type Eights naturally pair well with Nines.

In an Eight-Nine romantic partnership, the attraction factor is pretty high on both sides because a Nine is often drawn to strong personalities. The powerful, authoritative Eight, sometimes aggressive and forceful, likes to pair with a Nine. The Nine sees the high energy and competence radiated by an Eight as very appealing. They admire the Eight's ability to take on challenges. For an Eight, the appeal is more on the calmness of the Nine and how soothing their peaceful energy is to their relationship.

Type Nines naturally pair well with Ones and Twos.

As the peacemakers, their reassuring, harmonizing nature obviously draws in most Enneagram types.

In a Nine-One romantic partnership, the easy-going, peaceful nature of the Nine is very comforting and appealing to the type One. That inner critic and self-judgment are met with self-acceptance and gentleness from the Nine, which soothes anxiety and reduces the need to be right all the time. Likewise, the Nines benefit greatly in the structure, a sense of purpose, and clarity that a type One brings to their relationship.

In a Nine-Two romantic partnership, the loving and self-accepting Nine values and shows affection to the Two without taking advantage of them. They value the Two for who they are and not what they give. That's very comforting for a type Two who longs for that. Likewise, the Two's nurturing and attentive nature can help motivate the Nine into action. That takes him from that passive lethargic tendency into a more active and productive lifestyle.

None of these pairing types are set in stone. Often you might find success in same-type parings or even an Enneagram type that wasn't mentioned above. How much self-awareness you and your partner bring to the relationship matters. It's the determining factor of how fulfilling and healthy any relationship can be.

Now that you know your Enneagram number, wings and subtypes, start noticing how your instincts and motivations influence your reactions and behavior. Your temperament, early childhood, and unique experiences are ever-present when you begin a new relationship. Love is more than just that initial attraction. It's what happens after that initial "honeymoon" phase sizzles out. The more growth work you partake in together and individually, the better your chances of having a healthy and thriving relationship.

CHAPTER 13

HOW TO USE THE ENNEAGRAM AT WORK

As the business environment shifts and marketplace volatility increases, many organizations in the United States and abroad find it necessary to adjust their leadership and people management approaches. Technology, customer expectations, and many other factors add extra strain to employees of any business type and size. Smart business owners and employees are looking for different solutions that can enable them to improve productivity, teamwork, and emotional intelligence. The Enneagram has become one of those go-to tools for professionals who seek enlightenment, efficiency, and a better bottom line at their organization.

Why would businesses care about a tool that's rooted in ancient mysticism and spiritual teachings?

Understanding what drives people and discovering their strengths and weaknesses can influence company performance. In fact, it does impact performance way more than you think. If you are a leader or working within a team structure that seems to have plenty of gaps and incongruencies, this is one of the best ways to bring about positive change in the workplace. The Enneagram isn't about promoting a particular religious or psychological belief. Instead, it's about celebrating human diversity and prioritizing self-awareness and personal development as pre-requisite skills for professional growth.

BENEFITS OF USING THE ENNEAGRAM AT WORK

Healthy conflict resolution

Conflicts are part of a healthy team, and it's time we learn how to disagree respectfully. The Enneagram helps people come to a better understanding of their triggers, fears, motivations, and how to best communicate with others.

Greater meaning and productivity

As employees feel more cared for, valued, and understood at work, their commitment levels increase. In a 2017 Gallup study led by Dr. Amy Edmondson, they found that environments that improved their psychological safety experienced a 12% increase in productivity and less employee turnover. But fostering an environment where everyone feels safe and valued is hard if you don't have a tool like the Enneagram. What one employee perceives as a sign of care might threaten another depending on their Enneagram type. By deploying this tool across your organization, you will have clarity on the strategic moves to make that will ensure everyone experiences their version of "psychological safety."

Diversity and maximizing potential

After experimenting with the Enneagram tool, one of the core benefits different businesses have had is the ease by which the senior leadership can tap into each individual's uniqueness and highest potential. Accurately identifying where each person can be best positioned in a given project and allowing various types to tackle the same problem from different angles can maximize team contribution and performance.

EACH ENNEAGRAM TYPE AT WORK

We've already gone through the details of each Enneagram at a personal level. Now let's look at how you can relate to the various Enneagram Types in the workplace for better communication and team building.

Enneagram 1 - The Perfectionist

If you want to establish rapport with a type One, learn to respect their integrity and seriousness. Be a little more serious when interacting with them and know that they value the details that many of us tend to overlook.

To promote a healthy professional connection, engage in discussions of how things can be improved.

Avoid taking shortcuts or neglecting proper procedures when around Ones. It also doesn't hurt to keep good manners as they care a lot about doing things correctly. When making promises or arrangements, only agree to what you know you can see through to completion.

During conflicts, request them to be direct with their anger, so they don't harbor resentment. Genuinely acknowledge your mistake if you're in the wrong. Remember, Ones speaking style is precise and detail-oriented. When addressing them, do so with personal conviction and authority. If you know there's more than one right way, challenge them to see that too, but do it with kindness. When communicating with a One, always be clear about your expectations. Keep in mind they're trying to answer this unspoken question. "How can I fulfill my responsibility with integrity and in the perfect way?" Whatever you can do to support answering that question will go a long way in ensuring success.

Want to support their growth? If you're leading a type One, the best thing you can do is to encourage them to be less critical of themselves and more accepting of their mistakes and other people's seeming imperfections. You can also encourage them to share responsibilities with fellow team members and once in a while to just chill and have fun even while working on serious projects.

Enneagram 2 - The Helper

If you want to establish rapport with type Two, take the initiative and make that first contact. Regularly show your appreciation and approval.

To promote a healthy professional connection, encourage them to build partnerships and friendships that are warm and fulfilling for them.

Avoid being too critical, taking advantage of their generosity, or ignoring them as that deeply hurts their feelings. Twos are highly emotional, and it's essential for them that they are liked and accepted by others.

During conflicts, insist that they take responsibility for getting what they want instead of passing on the blame or evoking guilt. They tend to become resentful, so make sure to address that with as much empathy as you can. A Two's speaking style is sympathetic and nice. They love giving advice and being around a lot of people. Remember to regularly communicate your appreciation and say simple things like, "I really appreciate what you did there."

Want to support their growth? Encourage them to develop healthy boundaries and pay attention to their own needs and feelings.

Enneagram 3 - The Achiever

If you want to establish rapport with a type Three, acknowledge the hard work they put in. Be fast and efficient in your communication, so they don't feel like you're just wasting time.

To promote a healthy professional connection, become more proactive in the projects you work on together and focus on getting results.

Avoid getting in the way of their forward momentum. Threes have a lot of energy, and they can't stand failure or anyone hindering their success.

During conflicts, you have to be okay with getting a bit more aggressive in your exchanges, especially when things aren't going right. But don't let that deter you from staying on track with the overall goals. Threes are very enthusiastic, and they enjoy motivating themselves and others for success. Use that to your advantage in your communication. If you want them to get things done, offer incentives, including monetary rewards and public recognition. Threes can sometimes forget the value of people in the pursuit of success, so be assertive in reminding them that people have an essential role to play in success. Challenge their rhetoric while allowing them to save face when the situation calls for it.

Want to support their growth? Value them for who they are, not what they do, and make sure they know this. Encourage them to slow down once in a while and pay attention to their health. Create an atmosphere at work where failure is considered a good learning opportunity so they can stop demonizing it.

Enneagram 4 - The Individualist

If you want to establish rapport with a type Four, learn to vocalize your appreciation of their creativity and emotional sensitivity. Often these people are brilliant in their output and even if you may not agree with their art or sense of style, just acknowledge it.

To promote a healthy professional connection, value their individualism and effort into being unique and different.

Avoid making everything conform to logic and rationale if you want to win them over. They also don't enjoy doing status quo things, so try not to force them into conformity.

During conflicts, challenge the person to avoid withdrawing from the unresolved conversation and, at the same time, don't entertain their dramatic outbursts. The best you can do during disagreements is find a middle ground and refrain from taking everything they say to heart. Most of the time, type Fours say things they don't mean as their emotions run wild. Always remember that. A type Four's speaking style is sometimes warm and full of positive feelings, and sometimes it's dry and flat. To make your communication effective, I encourage you to validate and acknowledge their unique insights frequently. And try not to take their fluctuating moods personally.

Want to support their growth? Encourage healthy, respectful disagreements in your environment and let them know they are safe to express their emotions as long as they do so mindfully. Get them to watch what they say and consider the implications of their words and actions on others in the team. Promote mindfulness practices and self-awareness techniques that can enable them to create more emotional balance within and silence the inner critic.

Enneagram 5 - The Investigator

If you want to establish rapport with a type Five, be thoughtful in your approach and make sure you give them plenty of room to think and process information.

To promote a healthy professional connection, get together to discuss interests and deep and meaningful ideas. No small talk, please.

Avoid pressuring them into making immediate decisions or taking fast actions without proper thinking time.

During conflicts, you can agree to disagree with a Five. They are rational, technical, and can't stand chit-chat, which means they'll directly tell you what's going on if you ask the right way. Be mindful of signs of withdrawal, especially during a disagreement. When communicating, keep things professional and focused on their area of expertise. Give the person plenty of information and data, then allow them time to process. Don't pry into their personal life and if your business is flexible, consider allowing some flexibility in their work environment, e.g., remote work.

Want to support their growth? Encourage them to be warmer, generous and to forge strong relationships with a few key people in the team or organization. Make it safe for them to share as much or as little of their emotions as they feel comfortable doing. Remind the person that they need to let other team members know that they care but need plenty of alone time and space to work in solitude.

Enneagram 6 - The Loyalist

If you want to establish rapport with a type Six, make an effort to appreciate the natural tendency to worry and focus on problems. Let them know that you understand their need to guard and create a sense of safety. Agree on rules and procedures that aid in meeting that objective.

To promote a healthy professional connection, embrace their insights and acknowledge that you see value in dissecting all the worst-case scenarios before moving ahead with a given project.

Avoid changing rules too abruptly or withholding information from Sixes. As natural skeptics, lack of transparency or omission of critical details breeds doubts, leading to conflict.

During conflicts, don't be ambiguous. Speak clearly without discounting the person's concerns. At the same time, they refuse to take on their projections and insist that the individual takes responsibility for the situation at hand instead of creating external excuses. Sixes are naturally full of questions, so in your communication, let them know you are open to answering even the most tedious question as long as it helps put their mind at ease.

Want to support their growth? Sixes need a lot of psychological safety at work before mentally relaxing and stopping scanning for threats in every conversation. If you can create a "safe zone" where they can relax more, speak openly about their fears, and get reality checks without feeling judged, you're more likely to get the best out of this loyal individual.

The Enneagram 7 - The Enthusiast

If you want to establish rapport with a type Seven, learn to embrace their vibrant energy and enthusiasm for life. Learn to appreciate their endless stories and ideas.

To promote a healthy professional connection, encourage discussions that are fun, future-oriented, and filled with possibility.

Avoid being too negative or "reasonable" in your goal setting or ideas around Sevens. I also encourage you to always seek out various options for solving problems - challenge the Seven to help you find them.

During conflicts, challenge the person to take responsibility for their actions and insist on listening to other people's side of the story instead of talking over them. You might need to repeat this often. It's also important to be clear about what's expected and what the person should deliver because Sevens can easily get sidetracked. In your communication, switch it up a little when addressing a Seven and be more optimistic and excited about the project. But don't fake it.

Want to support their growth? The biggest support you can offer a Seven is to help them become a little more grounded and balanced between their constant desire for new and their ability to see things through before moving on to the next. Stress the importance of feedback and active listening, especially with fellow team members. Considering how much they hate pain, consider how you dish out negative feedback.

Enneagram 8 - The Challenger

If you want to establish rapport with a type Eight, make direct contact, be assertive, and don't back down in the face of their strength.

To promote a healthy professional connection, become proactive in helping them build momentum toward the desired result.

Avoid coming across as controlling or disrespectful. Given how energetic and domineering they are, I would avoid giving them assignments that cause them to sit still for too long.

During conflicts, you need to be bold enough to have healthy confrontations. Be authentic to yourself but deal with them directly and get ready to embrace the angry energy that's bound to come your way. Allow them to express their anger, but don't let it get out of hand. If they start to demonstrate destructive or violent behavior, do not stand for it at all. Since Eights are assertive speakers, they are more receptive to the same direct and bold communication style. Set clear goals, deadlines, and expectations in your communication, then leave them be. If you're savvy enough, figure out ways to plant ideas in their mind so they can "feel" more in control about taking the desired action. The more persuasive you are, the further you'll get with an Eight.

Want to support their growth? The best way to support type Eights is to figure out healthy ways for them to express their energy and emotions.

Enneagram 9 - Peacemaker

If you want to establish rapport with a type Nine, take time to listen, and I mean really listen to them. Encourage them to share what they care about so you can find common ground.

To promote a healthy professional connection, maintain peace. Nines cannot stand internal or external conflict, so if you can find ways to sustain a peaceful relationship at work, you'll win them over. It's that simple.

Avoid putting pressure on the person or making them feel bad for not moving as fast as the others. Of all the Enneagram types, Nines have the least energy, so their pace in execution is likely to be the slowest. Getting impatient or being too pushy will be counterproductive to your business goals.

During conflicts, do your best to demonstrate fairness in all matters. Find ways to disagree in healthy, non-threatening ways.

When dealing with a Nine, it pays to slow down and dig deeper, asking them to share what's really going on inside them. Sometimes a Nine will have an angry outburst or become passive-aggressive in their behavior. Let them know neither of these behaviors will be tolerated, and encourage them to work with you in resolving the issue. Nines speak with a lot of kindness and inclusivity. Try to use the right tone in your communication, so they don't interpret you as harsh and dismissive, leading to withdrawal. You should also establish clear priorities and give the person enough time to contemplate and process the task/assignment.

Want to support their growth? One of the best things you can do to support a Nine is to work with them to create structure and schedules around their work to keep them on track. Find small ways to constantly push them out of their comfort zone in ever so subtle ways so they can keep growing and contributing more to the organization.

PART FOUR
USING THE ENNEAGRAM FOR GROWTH IN ALL AREAS

CHAPTER 14

ACCELERATING YOUR PERSONAL GROWTH PART 1

Now that you've learned quite a bit about the Enneagram system and hopefully identified your personality type, what happens if you wish to change it? What if you're not happy with what you've discovered? What next? This is actually a pretty common experience, so don't worry if you're looking for answers on how to change your personality. Before I can give the long and short version answer, we should probably agree on a definition of personality.

Personality originates from the Latin word "persona," which refers to a theatrical mask that performers wear to project different roles during a play. Entertainers also used it to disguise their true identity during the performance. Your true identity is far grander, more real, and lasting than the persona that you're accustomed to wearing on a day-to-day basis. Based on that, let's agree that personality has nothing to do with who you really are.

And while at the most fundamental level, personality is about the thought patterns, feelings, and behaviors that make you unique, they are indeed not who you are. According to experts who study human personality, the consensus is that personality arises from within the individual and remains fairly constant throughout one's life. Enneagram experts seem to believe the same, which is why they say that an individual's Enneagram type cannot really change. To attempt to change your personality or your Enneagram type is a losing battle that I wouldn't encourage anyone to partake in. But all is not lost if you desire to grow and transform into a better version of yourself.

WHY PERSONALITY IS ALMOST IMPOSSIBLE TO CHANGE

Our personalities arise and are shaped based on many interacting factors that we can sum up into two broad categories - genetics and environment. Author and psychologists Carol Dweck asserts that, for the most part, our personalities are out of our control because even if we change the environment, genetics still influences us significantly. So if you're predisposed to being short-tempered and uptight but end up spending a long time in an environment that was zen-like and friendly, you'd likely see some shifts in your temperament to match that setting. Dweck often shares a story about twins to make this point. Two boys born identical twins were separated at birth. Raised in entirely different environments, one might expect no similar personality traits. As adults, however, the two men married women with the same first names, shared identical hobbies, and had similar levels of specific characteristics that experts could measure on personality assessments. Dweck proves the bias for the notion that we don't have control over our personality, but I do like that she continues to explore the solution that exists for those of us who desire change.

The secret to change and growth:

If you'd like to improve your current personality and the quality of your life, don't focus on what you cannot control, e.g., your Enneatype or genetics, and instead focus on what we know is within your control. And that is your behavior. Dweck believes that by changing habits, behavior patterns, and beliefs under the surface of your broad personality type, you can experience lasting personal transformation. That's where the Enneagram becomes super helpful because it gives you access to the aspects of you that lie beneath the surface of your overall personality. It also teaches you to move from a lower, underdeveloped version of your character to a higher and more "aligned" version of your personality. What do I mean by aligned? The alignment and connection between your personality and your higher self. After all, your real identity lies with your higher self rather than your persona. You have the ability to change your belief system, habits, coping strategies and close the gap that's responsible for all your anguish and restlessness.

HOW TO LEVERAGE THE ENNEAGRAM TOOL FOR POSITIVE CHANGE AND PERSONAL GROWTH

Embrace and accept your number

It's common to feel resistance about your Enneagram type once you've taken the test. If you're feeling uncomfortable and exposed, if perhaps you broke down in tears after reading some of the negative emotions and tendencies associated with your number, that's okay. I know it can feel intrusive, but the point of this quest is to bring awareness into your life and finally get to know who you are. Your personality type isn't better or worse than mine. Each Enneagram type is perfect as is and the best we can do is recognize, accept and make peace with where we are.

What we discover and uncover about ourselves shouldn't drown us in self-defeat or pity. It should empower us to consciously and purposely plot out how we'll approach the rest of our lives. All Enneagram types possess great strengths, unique offerings, and plenty of untapped potentials that can bring so much good into the world. Focus on unlocking more of that potential within yourself.

Identify the areas you'd like to improve

Now that you've accepted and embraced your Enneagram type, it's time to take an honest look at your life. Look at the state of your health, finances, career, mental and emotional well-being, relationships, and any other domain that matters to you. Where do you need to grow in the next 12 months? Is there a negative pattern you've identified that has to change? Are you looking to reconnect with your spiritual nature? Do you feel it's time to find your purpose or perhaps become more in-tune with your emotions? Whatever led you to pick up this book and study the Enneagram tool is the first thing you should improve. As you improve on one area and hone your skills, add more and more goals that bring you joy.

Put this knowledge into practice

It's one thing to read a book or attend a weekend seminar and an entirely different thing to put what you learn into practice. Many people who read this book will finish it proudly and pat themselves on the back. But unfortunately, they'll go back to doing exactly what they did before reading it and claim the book was a waste of time. The Enneagram and all the contents in this book work if you're willing to put in the effort and apply the lessons to your daily life.

The Enneagram tool shouldn't be used as a weapon to attack or manipulate others. It's meant to be used as a self-discovery tool so that as you understand yourself, you can meet others with more compassion. Instead of being at the mercy of your core fears and weaknesses, you can learn to tame them and still show up as the best version of yourself, even in the most challenging situations. When you catch yourself falling off track or reverting to old habits that no longer serve you, gently bring yourself back to focus without self-judgment or dwelling on past mistakes. This is the real purpose for the Enneagram teaching, and you can only reap the benefits when you apply the knowledge in your own life and track the progress you're making.

If you don't know what to focus on for your specific Enneagram type to see progress, let's break down some of the essential qualities you can cultivate, plus how to expedite your strengths.

ENNEAGRAM TYPE ONE - THE PERFECTIONIST – PATH TO GROWTH

Your essential qualities are integrity, goodness, and sacredness.

As you grow and awaken, the virtue you're moving toward realizing is serenity.

When it comes to accelerating your personal growth as a One, it's time to get deeply acquainted with your inner critic. That is, that little voice in your head that never shuts up. Ever measuring yourself up against certain ideals that are often unrealistic, it's easy to assume that becoming perfect is the way to self-actualization. Unfortunately, this couldn't be further from the truth. The way to use the Enneagram to accelerate growth and self-actualize is by focusing less on perfecting yourself—instead, practicing self-acceptance. Make an effort to relinquish the constant need for harsh judgment on yourself and others. It will transform you into a more compassionate, empathetic, and graceful person.

To bring you into a more serene and self-accepting state, here are some calming statements that can enable you to practice present moment awareness.

- *May I be at ease with myself.*
- *May I let go of judgments and forgive me and others knowing that this doesn't mean I agree with any particular behavior.*
- *May I be at ease with the things I consider imperfect realizing that serenity comes from knowing that the present moment is perfect just as it is.*

Once you've stabilized this way of thinking and feeling, here are some positive affirmations to add to your daily rituals.

- *I am at ease with life.*
- *I embrace myself completely.*
- *I am gentle with others.*
- *Everyone is doing the best they can at their current level of awareness, and I am accepting of this.*
- *I choose to be compassionate, understanding, and accepting of others.*
- *I forgive myself.*
- *Life is perfect as it is.*
- *I choose to be flexible, adaptable and embrace change.*

ENNEAGRAM TYPE TWO - THE HELPER – PATH TO GROWTH

Your essential qualities are love, affection, and nurture. The virtue you're moving toward as you grow and awaken is humility.

When it comes to accelerating your personal growth, it's time to stop people-pleasing and start tending to your own needs and living by example. The way to use the Enneagram to self-actualize is to invest time daily to get grounded within and to reconnect with your emotions first before jumping in to help others. Notice when feelings of pride push you to do things for others. And when the fear of being unloved tempts you to betray yourself and refuse to act from that perspective. Ask yourself regularly, "Am I tending to my own needs?" and "Is my giving authentic or set on expectations to get something in return?" Become emotionally present with yourself. Cultivate your confidence so you can start making the shift toward self-care and humility.

To begin walking the path of humility and unconditional love, here are some calming statements that can enable you to practice present moment awareness.

- *May I learn to love myself genuinely and see my own worth regardless of others' thoughts.*
- *May I give as much love to myself as I give to others.*
- *May I learn to give generously and authentically from a place of abundance.*
- *May I relinquish my send of pride and walk the path of humility.*

Once you've stabilized this way of thinking and feeling, here are some positive affirmations to add to your daily rituals.

- *I am loved for who I am.*
- *I am confident in myself.*
- *I have healthy emotional needs.*
- *I give sincerely from my heart.*
- *I establish healthy boundaries between myself and others.*

- *I feel accepted for who I am.*
- *I am able to express and ask for what I want.*

ENNEAGRAM TYPE THREE - THE ACHIEVER – PATH TO GROWTH

Your essential qualities are value, glory, and preciousness. The virtue you're moving toward as you grow and awaken is authenticity.

When it comes to accelerating your personal growth, focus less on status and the mask you wear in public and more on your true self. Creating an illusion of what you think will make others perceive you as successful is counterproductive in the long run and will lead to the very things you fear. Instead, lean into your truth, strength, and ability to do more than others. But do so from a holistic place where your emotional needs aren't sacrificed. Embrace your natural leadership qualities and, at the same time, cultivate rich relationships. Regularly check in with your feelings and give yourself downtime to reset when needed.

To begin walking the path of practicing present moment awareness, here are some calming statements.

- *May I cultivate stillness and reconnect with my true feelings.*
- *May I allow greater patience into my day.*
- *May I have compassion in the face of suffering for myself and others.*

Once you've stabilized this way of thinking and feeling, here are some positive affirmations to add to your daily rituals.

- *I am open to acknowledging my feelings.*
- *I am enough.*

- *I inspire leadership in others.*
- *I am loved by others who appreciate me as I am.*
- *I am aligned with my true self.*
- *I am ready to acknowledge the efforts of my team.*
- *I celebrate the accomplishments of others.*

CHAPTER 15

ACCELERATING YOUR PERSONAL GROWTH PART 11

ENNEAGRAM TYPE FOUR - THE INDIVIDUALIST – PATH TO GROWTH

Your essential qualities are beauty, intimacy, depth, and mystery. The virtue you're moving toward as you grow and awaken is equanimity.

When it comes to accelerating your personal growth, it's time to stop clinging to the brokenness you see in the world and start becoming the solution. Embody what you see is lacking or missing in the world. Perhaps as a child, you craved compassion and just leadership. Now that you're an adult, it's time to cultivate those qualities so you can become the change you wish to see in the world. Use the Enneagram tool to practice self-love and reconnect with your true identity. Finding your true self and feeling deeply loved matter to you, and rightly so, the knowledge of the Enneagram can enable you to finally realize that you're not broken, and finding yourself can only be accomplished by going within. Take time to notice and catch yourself when you start dwelling on what's missing or lacking. Bring yourself to the present moment. Cultivate high self-esteem and practice a little more enthusiasm. It will do you a world of good to allow your feelings to spin over to the good side of life.

To begin walking the path of equanimity and gratitude, here are some calming statements that can enable you to practice present moment awareness.

- *May I delight in the happiness of others.*
- *May I learn to appreciate what is rather than dwell on what isn't.*
- *May I appreciate and rejoice in myself as I increase my awareness about how life really works.*
- *May I learn to treat all beings with equal and positive regard.*

Once you've stabilized this way of thinking and feeling, here are some positive affirmations to add to your daily rituals.

- *I am centered in my true essence.*
- *I draw on my gifts to inspire the world.*
- *I am more than my emotions and my human experience.*
- *I choose to live in the present moment.*
- *I choose to release the past and find grace.*
- *I am happy to be me.*

ENNEAGRAM TYPE FIVE - THE INVESTIGATOR – PATH TO GROWTH

Your essential qualities are clarity, illumination, insight, and solitude. The virtue you're moving toward as you grow and awaken in nonattachment.

When it comes to accelerating your growth, it's time to take action and use your vastly deep knowledge and understanding to pinpoint which changes need to be made in the world. Allow your competence to serve your mission rather than making your research and knowledge the mission. You have the ability to do great things and positively impact the world, and it's time to lean more into this ability. Use the Enneagram tool to enable you to embrace the physical world so you can channel more insight. Freely offer your knowledge without fear. Learn to make the distinction between knowledge, wisdom, and insight.

To begin walking the path of openness, nonattachment, and being in the flow of the universe, here are some calming statements that can enable you to practice present moment awareness.

- *May I realize that the universe is abundant.*
- *May I feel secure within myself and trust that I will receive what I need.*
- *May I be at peace with not knowing, all the while realizing I already have ample knowledge.*
- *May I open my heart to engage fully in life's energy.*

Once you've stabilized this way of thinking and feeling, here are some positive affirmations to add to your daily rituals.

- *I am grounded in my being.*
- *I am calm, serene, and at peace even amidst life uncertainties.*
- *I thrive well in this world.*
- *I choose to connect with others.*
- *I experience life fully.*
- *I develop healthy relationships with the people around me.*
- *I appreciate the awe of being in my body.*
- *I have general trust in the people around me.*

- *I love myself.*
- *I feel abundant.*

ENNEAGRAM TYPE SIX - THE LOYALIST – PATH TO GROWTH

Your essential qualities are truth, guidance, and intuition. The virtue you're moving toward as you grow and awaken is courage.

When it comes to accelerating your growth, it's time to realize that your constant search for trustworthiness and security is actually concealing your insecurities. In the long run, it becomes counterproductive because the fear only grows. Use the Enneagram tools to finally address the internal insecurities. Understand that your imagination tends to dramatize situations, so catch yourself and notice this is a blind spot whenever you get trapped in a worst-case scenario. Then act accordingly, leaning more into the situation with curiosity rather than fearfully running away from the situation or person because most of the time, nothing is as bad as you see it in your imagination. As you get better at using the Enneagram tool and teaching, you will trust more in your inner guidance and let go of fear patterns.

To begin walking the path of courage, here are some calming statements that can enable you to practice present moment awareness.

- *May I turn fear into a friend instead of becoming victimized and imprisoned by its story.*
- *May I cultivate courage instead of constantly changing after security and certainty.*
- *May I have faith in myself and in life itself.*
- *May I learn to live more in the present moment and notice my tendency to magnify situations.*

Once you've stabilized this way of thinking and feeling, here are some positive affirmations to add to your daily rituals.

- *I am calm and centered.*
- *I choose to trust myself and my inner guidance.*
- *I am well supported by my team members and friends.*
- *My inner counsel is wise.*
- *I love myself.*
- *The world is a safe place, and the universe supports me.*
- *I make independent and clear decisions for myself.*

ENNEAGRAM TYPE SEVEN - THE ENTHUSIAST – PATH TO GROWTH

Your essential qualities are joy, hope, and freedom. The virtue you're moving toward as you grow and awaken is sobriety.

When it comes to accelerating your personal growth, the best you can do is increase your curiosity about what it truly means to be free. The tendency is to seek out growth and freedom by pursuing a new challenge, adventure, or opportunity. Unfortunately, this rarely leads to the change you truly crave. Use the Enneagram tool to go within and increase your understanding of yourself. Dive deep into the nature of being and find your lasting freedom there. Learn to process both positive and negative emotions.

To begin walking the path of sobriety and emotional mastery, here are some calming statements that can enable you to practice present moment awareness.

- *May I allow myself to feel all my emotions, including sadness, suffering, and sorrow, and reflect without being judgmental or harsh on myself.*
- *May I have compassion for myself and all other beings.*

- *May I learn to find freedom from within, which will allow me to have freedom in everything I do, even when it's mundane or repetitive.*
- *May I learn to find joy in the present moment ordinary activities.*

Once you've stabilized this way of thinking and feeling, here are some positive affirmations to add to your daily rituals.

- *I am abundant.*
- *I am content, fulfilled, and joyful.*
- *I am free to express who I am.*
- *I am grounded in my being and engaged in all I do.*
- *I am in touch with my emotions and inner guidance.*
- *I find joy in the present moment.*
- *I choose to focus my energy and attention.*

ENNEAGRAM TYPE EIGHT - THE CHALLENGER – PATH TO GROWTH

Your essential qualities are strength, aliveness, and power. The virtue you're moving toward as you grow and awaken is innocence.

When it comes to accelerating your growth, it's not about giving up your desired challenges and taking massive action. It's about getting into alignment first. The need to control everything and impose your will over others tends to be more counterproductive than helpful for your development. You also struggle with the belief that vulnerability means weakness, but the truth is, allowing yourself to be vulnerable, especially to your closest relationships, will only make you stronger. To be truly courageous and strong, one must also tune with their emotions.

As a natural leader, your powerful, authoritative and decisive instincts will be amplified as you use the Enneagram tool to get in tune with your emotional side. It will also enable you to be more open to receiving counsel from the person you most love who is also looking out for your well-being. Instead of being dismissive, pause for a moment and become more receptive. Listen with both your head and heart before rejecting input from a loved one.

To begin walking the path of innocence, here are some calming statements that can enable you to practice present moment awareness.

- *May I learn to embody gentleness and compassion.*
- *May I be receptive to the truth in all beings.*
- *May I cultivate more of a growth mindset and the innocence of a beginner's mind so I can enter each new situation with a fresh perspective.*

Once you've stabilized this way of thinking and feeling, here are some positive affirmations to add to your daily rituals.

- *I am peaceful and calm.*
- *I am in touch with my emotional needs.*
- *I respect the decision of others.*
- *I am sensitive to the needs of others.*
- *I can be gentle and firm at the same time.*
- *I practice patience.*
- *I embrace every part of me, including what I perceive as weakness.*

ENNEAGRAM TYPE NINE - THE PEACEMAKER – PATH TO GROWTH

Your essential qualities are harmony, wholeness, and interconnectedness. The virtue you're moving toward as you grow and awaken is engagement.

The best gift you can give to the world is using your natural ability to create peace and wholeness in your relationships. But to do that, you'll need to activate more of your innate powers and embody the solutions that others are struggling to see. When it comes to accelerating your personal growth, it's time to stop going along with things or blending in when you know it's not of the highest good just to avoid conflict. Do your best to notice when the resistance kicks in, and you withdraw simply because you want to avoid creating conflict by stating your truth. Cultivate the courage to speak up and find healthy ways to deal with disagreements. Use the Enneagram tool to help you notice your unproductive habits and tendency to revert to passive-aggressive behavior instead of boldly speaking up and actively working out solutions to problems. Allow the knowledge gained from the study of the Enneagram to aid you in exploring the underlying message that causes you to withdraw and ignore your own voice.

To begin walking the path of wholeness and right action, here are some calming statements that can enable you to practice present moment awareness.

- *May I discover my purpose and live more intentionally.*
- *May I become more aware of my inertia toward myself, knowing that the right action comes from valuing myself the same as I value others.*
- *May I focus on what's important, especially in the face of discomfort and conflict.*

- *May I remember my priorities and values.*

Once you've stabilized this way of thinking and feeling, here are some positive affirmations to add to your daily rituals.

- *I am peaceful and whole.*
- *I can honor my voice and speak my truth even when it's not comfortable.*
- *I can bring a healing presence to others without neglecting myself.*
- *I am loved just as I am.*
- *I am grateful, and I actively participate in the joys of daily living.*
- *I acknowledge and value my own identity.*

CHAPTER 16

UNLOCKING YOUR POTENTIAL AND A FULFILED LIFE

W ill you choose to live the Enneagram? Too many people get stuck in the theory and study of this wonderful system. That's quite unfortunate because, without daily practice and integration, the teachings of the Enneagram can never translate into results. A significant weakness in personality tests and personal development is the lack of emphasis on practicing what one learns.

I see the Enneagram as one of the best tools for shifting perspectives about life, our past, present, and future. The Enneagram tool enables us to discover more of who we really are. It's all about growth and development, helping us embody what makes us distinctly who we are. Our personal and professional lives benefit greatly when we begin to show up more as our true selves. Use the Enneagram model as a map that points you in the direction of your highest and best self. Take note of your strengths and weaknesses, so you can make better choices as you continue to navigate life.

HOW DO YOU WANT THE NEXT 12 MONTHS TO PLAY OUT?

Regardless of external factors or what the news tells you, the next year can be whatever you choose it to be. That's because you have control over your mind and, in turn, how you'll navigate experiences and circumstances. Think about this: No matter what's going on with the government or economy, some people will struggle tremendously, and some will succeed tremendously. Even during a crisis, some people continue to thrive. Wouldn't it be nice if you could be among those that thrive in all seasons?

The key to ensuring the next twelve months are significantly different from the last lies within you. You can use the Enneagram to help you unlock all the dormant power and potential that remains unutilized so that you can finally take charge of your life. This doesn't mean striving for more, hustling more, or forcing things into place. The more self-aware you become of both your conditioned limitations and untapped opportunities, the easier it will be to make the right choices for your life.

So far, we've gone through personal growth recommendations for each Enneagram type. Go back and re-read as much as you can about your Enneagram type and the simple action steps you can take to move your life forward. Besides understanding what your specific Enneagram type needs and wants to continue developing in healthy ways, there are some universal practices that will work for all of us regardless of our type. Some are ancient practices passed on by spiritual teachers and sages, while others are scientifically researched and discovered. Pick a handful of practices from this list, make them a daily habit and commit to living the Enneagram, not just studying it.

PRACTICES AND TECHNIQUES YOU SHOULD KNOW ABOUT

Cultivate Self-love

We've mentioned self-love several times throughout this book. But most people tend to misunderstand what it means. It's not just about feeling good or taking time to rest and self-care. Self-love is much deeper and more fundamental than that. It's a state of total awe and appreciation for oneself that grows from the actions that support your physical, psychological and spiritual growth. Self-love is one of the most important practices you can incorporate into your daily life if you live the Enneagram. It enables you to accept both strengths and weaknesses, meet your failures with compassion, and find personal meaning and fulfillment in life. When viewed through the lens of self-love, your life and the world takes on a different tone, one that's more in harmony with universal laws. How you see the world and interpret others doesn't come from outside, it comes from inside. The lower your self-love levels, the darker your vision, and conversely, the higher your self-love, the brighter your vision.

HOW DOES ONE BEGIN TO CULTIVATE SELF-LOVE?

As with all good things in life, it's a matter of forming a habit. Take small steps daily to reconnect with your whole self, nurturing and tending to your physical, psychological, and spiritual needs. Over time, those small actions will add up into habits that become your new norm. You must also notice how you communicate with yourself. Is your inner dialogue constantly negative? Are you often doubting, berating, and betting against yourself? The more time you spend compassionately checking in with yourself, the easier it will be to catch and prune all the unruly thoughts and emotions.

Forgiveness as a practice

One of the best tools you can use in this journey of self-discovery is the practice of daily forgiveness. Realize that forgiveness doesn't mean abdicating responsibility or even justifying a wrong. It simply means giving yourself (or another) compassion and shifting your perspective from how things are to how you'd like it to be. Why would you need to do this? Because your point of power will always be in the present moment. But each time you're holding on to any blame or resentment, you're stuck in the past. It robs you of your power and takes you off the path of living the Enneagram.

Here's the thing, you'll make many mistakes on this journey, and you'll also realize how much your ignorance has hurt you and others. Once we realize how short we've fallen from our true potential, we tend to self-loathe and self-punish. That is the worst move for us to make. The right thing to do is to exercise forgiveness. Learn to practice self-compassion when you fall short of whom you want to be. The same is true for those you feel have ill-treated you. As Louise Hay says, " No matter how justified you feel you are, no matter what "they" did, if you insist on holding on to the past, then you'll never be free."

A few statements to practice forgiveness:

- *I forgive myself for not being perfect. I know I am doing my best and living the very best way I know-how.*
- *I forgive everyone in my past and present for all perceived wrongs. I release all people with love.*
- *I love and approve of myself.*

Gratitude

Equally as important as practicing forgiveness daily regardless of your Enneagram type is the habit of feeling grateful. Humans have a negative bias (I can't tell you why, but we tend to remember bad things more than the good in our lives). That means that you're likely to dwell on your inadequacies or problems or things that are going wrong far longer than dwelling on everything that's going well. The antidote to this bias is gratitude.

Gratitude transforms our everyday experiences (personal and professional) into more positive and enjoyable experiences. There's compelling evidence showing that the daily practice of gratitude makes everyone feel better and positively impacts their health, creativity, relationships, and productivity. Use gratitude to neutralize your brain's negativity bias and as a tool to enable you to live the Enneagram model. Start by picking a time of day (first thing in the morning or last thing before sleep time) to write down three to five things that you feel grateful for on that particular day.

Make an effort to find unique things to praise and appreciate, no matter how small. Some mornings the thing I am most grateful for is the sound of a bird singing outside my window as I wake up. Other days I'm just so thankful for the air that I breathe. Find magic in the things you often take for granted, and it will enable you to understand what life is all about in more profound ways.

Mindfulness practices

Many people hear the word "mindfulness" and immediately assume it means sitting in silent meditation with a blank mind. That's a very limited view of what mindfulness means. Whether you enjoy meditating or not, adding mindfulness practices to your daily routines at home and work will be instrumental to your growth. Unless you can figure out ways of bringing that mindfulness factor into your activities, you won't experience the full benefits of being mindful. But how can one become mindful in the context of a busy workday or a demanding lifestyle?

Choose to be more present in your life. Take it moment by moment, hour-by-hour at first, until it turns into a habit. Mindfulness is not about blanking out your mind. It's about being intentional as you move through your life. It's about becoming more aware of your mind, environment, and inner world.

When you're absent-minded at work or during a meeting (or a date), you're lacking mindfulness, and that's when pre-programmed impulses usually step in and wreak havoc. Functioning on autopilot isn't always a good thing, especially if you're looking to create new changes in your life. So here's an idea that can help you stop being mindless in professional and personal settings. Choose to train yourself into present-moment awareness. Each morning before you start interacting with the world, decide with the intention that you're going to be as present as you can in all your activities. Pause for a few minutes before switching from one activity to another and remind yourself of this decision. For example, when you enter your car to drive to work, decide that you will only focus on that activity. Keep yourself grounded in that present moment by listening to the sound of your car's engine as you accelerate. Notice how your hands feel against the leather and how tight or relaxed your grip is. Pay attention to what's in front of you and around your as you drive. Try to notice things you wouldn't usually look too keenly at, such as how long it takes the traffic lights to switch or how fast the lady crossing the pedestrian walk in front of you is moving. Avoid thinking about Helen and her new promotion or John's tendency to procrastinate on projects.

When you get to work, before getting into your boss's office, intentionally pause and remind yourself to be as present as possible with them. If you take this intention with you into every activity, sooner or later, you will start to see some changes.

What if I struggle to remember to practice mindfulness?

Use the tools at your disposal to keep you accountable. Set the alarm on your phone so that at least three times a day, you pause for 30seconds to "check-in" and see how well you're doing. If you're at work, make sure the alarm only vibrates, so it doesn't constantly nag others. Each time the alarm goes off, excuse yourself and find a moment of silence at the balcony, bathroom, or your office. Take a deep mindful breath. Notice how you're feeling. Reflect on how the day is going so far. Were you acting from your highest level of awareness? Are you noticing patterns of thought or impulsive, emotional reactions that perhaps need to be addressed during your free time? The more self-aware you can be, the easier it will be to reclaim the self-control and self-mastery you seek.

CONCLUSION

Finally, you come to the end of this first step in what will be a lifelong quest of self-discovery. By now, it should be evident that living the Enneagram is your surest path to the freedom, sense of unity, and the sense of wholeness you've been seeking all your life. You have learned your Enneagram type and the richness of the wings, subtypes, and triad that the model teaches. And you've also learned about your virtue and the inner calling from your spirit. Should you choose to pursue that path of spiritual awakening, you'll need to continue developing yourself and bravely dive deeper and deeper into the study of the Enneagram model.

Understanding yourself better should also equip you with the ability to understand others better and show more empathy and compassion. Remember, everyone is fighting a hard battle as they strive to find that unity of being and heal their ego fixations and passions. The filter through which others view the world determines why you notice their reactions and behaviors to be as they are. Suppose you desire to establish and strengthen rich nourishing relationships. In that case, it's essential to keep in mind that their level of development and current level of awareness limits them to act as they do. Your responsibility is to forgive, embrace and practice acceptance. Since you know how to be and do better, thanks to your investment in the teachings of the Enneagram, step up and be that shining example in the relationship.

Growing into your best self is ultimately what living the Enneagram is all about. And while you cannot change from one type to another, there's so much room for you to grow and more than enough potential for you to unlock. Once you discover all the magnificence you possess, you'll never want to be any other type. Even more remarkable is how the Enneagram tool enables us to transform professional and personal relationships. With your newfound understanding of yourself and others, you'll have a better grasp of why one person behaves as they do and others don't. But that doesn't mean you'll have all the answers to why your boss is so aggressive in meetings or why your new girlfriend wants you hitting the clubs every weekend. What you'll have is a better understanding of the motivations behind these behaviors.

Another critical thing to remember is that you can't assume anyone's Enneagram type - that's for them to figure out. If you're in a leadership position at work and can advocate for everyone to take the test, then great. Only after the person confirms their actual Enneagram type can you approach them in the manner directed in this book. Don't pressure anyone to take the test, especially not your romantic partner. It has to be something the person wants to do.

Once you surround yourself with people who know their Enneagram type and are willing to improve themselves just as you are, what's next? Well, keep growing, learning, and experimenting with developing even further. There's no end to living the enneagram knowledge. But there are two last nuggets I will leave for you.

First, be easy on yourself. Embrace both the positive and negative things you discovered going through this book. You started reading it for a reason. You wanted to know yourself better, and now you're well on the way to self-mastery. Take deep breaths, one day at a time, and cultivate one new habit at a time as you soak in this information. The human journey is full of speed bumps and unforeseen obstacles, but as long as you give yourself the grace to get back up when you fall, the journey will be fulfilling. If you're an Enneagram One, this might be hard to hear because you want everything perfect all the time. Keep working on that inner critic so you can go a little easy on yourself. I know you can do it. For Enneagram Two, being easy on yourself would mean investing time in self-care, not just tending to the needs of others. Enneagram Three, as hard as this might be for you, it's time to recognize that success isn't just about accomplishing stuff. Don't be too hard on yourself. Enneagram Four constantly remind yourself that there are those who get you and love you in all your uniqueness, and they wouldn't change a thing about you. Be easy on yourself as you find those people to connect with and learn to see the good in you.

Enneagram Five, this world sorely needs your knowledge and ingenuity, but please be more open and gentle with yourself. Be easy with your emotions and find the value in having a rich relationship with another. Enneagram Six, your anxiety, worry, and mistrust does get the best of you all too often, but no matter how many times you catch yourself falling, dust yourself up and keep moving forward. Identify your triggers, and with time you'll counteract them. Enneagram Seven, I know negativity, pain, and suffering feel unbearable. Still, I promise you, if you practice sitting with that emotions and processing them (allowing them to flow just as a river would), you'll eventually crack that aspect of you as well. Enneagram Eight, be patient with yourself toward the road of embracing vulnerability. It's not easy, but I know you are strong enough to do it. Enneagram Nine, I know conflict is challenging for you but find the courage to face uncomfortable conversations and speak your truth. Be easy during this process and start slowly.

The second and final word of wisdom that I encourage you to do regardless of your Enneagram type is to be easy on others. Compassion and empathy are sorely lacking in our population, and it's time we take steps to cultivate them personally. Now that you know how different types interact in relationships, their driving motivations, and behaviors, is it too much to ask for a little more patience and empathy? I am not suggesting you excuse or even accept bad behavior. But I insist that we increase our tolerance and understanding for each other. Forgiveness becomes the magic ingredient here. As you learn to forgive yourself and others, you will find better, more humane ways to communicate and get along with others. That is the kind of growth we should all aim for because it fosters the kind of future that promotes a healthy population. May the Enneagram tool guide you on this journey of becoming your best version.

Enjoy the journey of awakening to your true Self.

Dan Davis.

RESOURCES

Enneagram Tests Online:

Enneagram. (n.d.). The Enneagram Institute. Retrieved January 17, 2022, from https://tests.enneagraminstitute.com/

The Enneagram Personality Test. (2021, October 25). Truity. Retrieved January 17, 2022, from https://www.truity.com/test/ enneagram-personality-test

Other useful resources:

Traditional Enneagram (History). (n.d.). The Enneagram Institute. Retrieved January 17, 2022, from https://www.enneagraminsti tute.com/the-traditional-enneagram/

Christian, K. (2021, October 20). *How To Cultivate Healthier Relationships Based On Your Enneagram Type.* The Good Trade. Retrieved January 17, 2022, from https://www.thegoodtrade.com/ features/enneagram-in-relationships

Yuan, L. (2021, August 23). *Breaking Down the Enneagram: A Guide for Total Beginners.* Truity. Retrieved January 17, 2022, from https://

www.truity.com/blog/breaking-down-enneagram-guide-total-beginners

SAGE Journals: Your gateway to world-class research journals. (n.d.). SAGE Journals. Retrieved January 17, 2022, from https://journals.sagepub.com/action/cookieAbsent

www.ingramcontent.com/pod-product-compliance
Lightning Source LLC
Chambersburg PA
CBHW032053020426
42335CB00011B/313